Life Together in the Spirit:

A Radical Spirituality for the Twenty-First Century

John Driver

Institute for the Study of Global Anabaptism
Goshen College
Goshen, Ind.

GOSHEN COLLEGE
INSTITUTE FOR THE STUDY OF GLOBAL ANABAPTISM

Copyright © 2011 Institute for the Study of Global Anabaptism
Goshen College
1700 S. Main St.
Goshen, IN 46526

isga@goshen.edu
www.goshen.edu/institutes/anabaptism

Translated from *Convivencia Radical: Espiritualidad para el siglo 21*
with permission from Kairós Ediciones

Cover design: Adriana Vázquez
Editor: John D. Roth
Layout/Design: Penina Christine Acayo

First English edition 2011
All rights reserved.
ISBN 978-0-9837094-0-4

The translation and distribution of this book was made possible
through a grant from Greencroft Communities, given to
recognize the talents and spiritual gifts of Greencroft Goshen
resident, John Driver. This gift is part of Greencroft's efforts to
further the mission and ministry of the broader Mennonite and
Christian church.

GREENCROFT COMMUNITIES

CONTENTS

Life Together in the Spirit

FOREWORD

When the history of the Christian church is written at some future time, the twentieth century could well be labeled the "Century of the Holy Spirit." In North America, the Asuza Street Revival of 1906, which gave rise to the Pentecostal movement, was followed at mid-century by a wave of charismatic renewal that left its mark on nearly every denomination. During the last decades of the century, Pentecostal churches in countries around the world have experienced explosive growth, transforming the face of the global Christian church. Today, Pentecostalism is the fastest growing branch of the Christian church, with the overwhelming majority of its adherents residing in Africa, Latin America, and parts of Asia, Although estimates vary, there are now some 250 million Pentecostals in the global church, a figure that rises to nearly 2 billion if you include all those who consider themselves to be "charismatic Christians."

These new expressions of Christian spirituality have had enormous consequences for the church. Contrary to the assumptions of many Western sociologists—who had confidently predicted that modern forces of secularism would soon make Christian faith obsolete—the Pentecostal and charismatic renewal movements have brought renewed energy, vitality, and life to many parts of the Christian church, and have enabled millions of believers to experience genuine physical, emotional, and spiritual healing.

But the resolute focus on the presence and power of the Holy Spirit has also opened the church to some distortions of the gospel message. Many forms of contemporary Christian spirituality, for example, are intensely individualistic, and even self-centered. And modern understandings of the Spirit also tend to define the "spiritual" as an abstract, mysterious, ethereal reality, sharply separated from ethical practices or the shared life of the Christian community. To be sure, spirit-filled Christians continue to gather in churches for singing, vigorous preaching and dramatic healing services, but the primary focus of the Christian life is often centered on the personal experience of the individual believer. Thus, Christian discipleship can easily be subordinated to the emotional experience of the Spirit's presence; and the church becomes merely a tool for helping individuals achieve their desired goals, often framed as personal "health and wealth."

In this book, John Driver draws on more than 50 years of experience as a missionary, historian, theologian, teacher, and pastor to offer a fresh understanding of spirituality from biblical and historical perspective. Driver has spent a lifetime ministering to pastors, congregations and renewal movements in Spanish-speaking settings shaped both by the profound historical influence of Catholicism and by the more recent influence of Protestant evangelicals and Pentecostalism. This book, originally published as *Convivencia Radical: Una Espiritualidad para el Siglo XXI*, undoubtedly reflects the Hispanic context of its origins. At the same time, however, Driver's reflections on Christian spirituality transcend any particular culture—and they may be especially relevant for Mennonite churches in North America who are seeking spiritual renewal by borrowing heavily from evangelical sources.

As you will quickly discover, the living presence of the Holy Spirit is at the core of Driver's understanding of Christian faith. Yet careful biblical study and historical reflection have led him to an interpretation of the Spirit's role in the Christian life— deeply anchored in the life and teachings of Jesus and in the example of the early church—that is markedly different from many other contemporary expressions of spirituality. At the heart of Driver's argument, is a deep affirmation of the Incarnation, the "word made flesh." God has revealed Himself most fully to humanity in the person of Jesus Christ, who came to this earth not only as a judge, or as an expiation for human sin, but also as "the new Adam" who restores a fallen creation to its original purpose. In Christ, Christians can become part of a "new creation" (I Cor. 5:16), in which the traditional divisions between word and deed, spirit and flesh, mission and ethics, become incomprehensible.

For Driver, "being spiritual" has less to do with one's inner emotional state than whether we are being transformed into the likeness of Christ, participating in his ministry of healing and reconciliation, as well as in his self-giving love for the world which ultimately led to his death and resurrection. Far from being a private experience, the Spirit is made visible in the world in the gathered body of believers, united by baptism, and committed to giving and receiving counsel, sharing material possessions, and suffering for others, even as Christ has suffered on our behalf.

This understanding of the Spirit, Driver argues, was at the heart of the early church's witness to the world; and it also found expression in the sixteenth-century radical renewal movement known as Anabaptism. Thus, the book offers a great introduction to Anabaptist-Mennonite understandings of the Christian faith, even as it explores the deeper Christian tradition and opens the door to genuine conversation with other Christian groups.

*   *   *   *

Life Together in the Spirit is the first publication of the Institute for the Study of Global Anabaptism, an initiative of Goshen College, which has among its objectives the renewal of the church in North America through a deeper understanding of the rapidly growing Anabaptist-Mennonite movement in the global south. It is fitting that we inaugurate that series with a book by John Driver. Although his name evokes immediate recognition in Anabaptist circles virtually anywhere in Mexico, Central

America, South America, or Spain, Driver's gifts to the church have not yet been fully appreciated in North America. In Spanish-speaking contexts, Driver is widely known for the profound simplicity and clarity of his teaching. But beyond that, he is known as a person whose very life—in his generosity, simplicity, gracious spirit, and evident love for all God's people—embodies the message of his teachings.

In this sense, Driver reflects in his personal life what he yearns for in the church. That is, a witness to the living presence of the Spirit made known not because the church *has* a message, but because the church, in the quality of its life together, *is* a message. If the Spirit of the living God does not find tangible expression in the Body of Christ—if the good news of the gospel is not evident in transformed relations—the church is likely building on a foundation of sand.

In addition to expressing my deep thanks to John, it is also pleasure to recognize the crucial role that Steve Slagel, pastor of East Goshen Mennonite Church, played in supporting translation and publication of this volume, written by a beloved member of his congregation. Finally, I am also pleased to acknowledge the significant support provided by Greencroft Communities, and especially its president and CEO, Mark King, in helping to honor one of Greencroft's active members through the translation of this book.

May this text encourage Christians of all backgrounds, in every part of the world, to embrace a fresh understanding of the Spirit in all of its fullness, so that the Body of Christ may indeed be made visible in the world today. And may all who encounter that Spirit be transformed in every aspect of their life.

– John D. Roth, Director

Institute for the Study of
Global Anabaptism
Goshen (Ind.) College

Current and Planned Programs

Conferences/Seminars that bring international guests into conversation with the North American church

May Term "Global Anabaptist History" (on location in various countries)

Student Scholarship (linked to internships in the MHL or MQR – training future Anab.-Menn. scholars)

Faculty Development in Anabaptist-Mennonite theology and pedagogy

Building on the unique resources of the MHL
fraternal exchange focused on the global
•le and vibrant point of intersection connecting
stian church.

PROLOGUE

Radical Ecclesiology:
Doing Justice and Building Peace as Faithful Minority Movements

"Do not follow the crowd in doing wrong . . . Do not pervert justice by siding with the crowd." (Ex. 23:2, NIV)

"Anyone who does not do what is right is not a child of God; neither is anyone who does not love his brother." (1 Jn. 3:10, NIV)

From the middle of the fourth century until early in the sixteenth century the only way of being a Christian and a member of the Christian church was to be a Roman Catholic — that is, through unquestioning conformity with the magisterial authority of the Catholic church and ultimately its head, the Pope.

However, throughout this millennium of church history there were many Christians who gave witness to an underlying tradition of nonconformity, even though they were obliged to conform to the official system. These Christians were well aware of the enormous gap between the enslaving obligations demanded by the religious system of their time and the transforming, liberating teachings of Jesus of Nazareth.

As faithful minority movements, these small nonconforming groups tried in a variety of ways to change the prevailing realities of their time. But the intolerant rigidity of the teachings and structures of the Catholic church during these centuries made it impossible for their discordant voices to be heard. Relationships within the Christian church were not characterized

ix

by the practice of love that Jesus taught his followers. To the contrary, those who advocated for radical changes were effectively silenced through persecution, torture, exile or death.

On October 31, 1517, the German Augustinian monk and university professor, Martin Luther, challenged the established order by publicly protesting what he and many others of his time considered to be serious spiritual, theological and pastoral misdeeds of the Catholic church. The German princes supported his initiative with their political power, marking the beginnings of the Protestant Reformation of the sixteenth century.

The Catholic church of the late Middle Ages refused to tolerate this kind of reform in its midst. Thus, Luther was persecuted and excommunicated, and his followers—whom he called "evangelicals" because of their professed loyalty to the Gospel—were mockingly identified as "Protestants."

The Protestant Reformation has sometimes also been called the "Magisterial Reformation" due to the significant role that "magistrates"—city councils, princes and kings—played in supporting reformers like Martin Luther, Ulrich Zwingli and John Calvin. The principal denominations that arose out of the Magisterial Reformation were the Lutheran and the Reformed churches. The Church of England, or the Anglican church, was also influenced by the Protestant Reformation on the European continent. Later, in Scotland, the Presbyterian church emerged, as yet another fruit of the Reformation.

Almost immediately, however, individual members in these churches, as well as within Catholicism, began to point out that the Protestant Reformation had been only partial. Under the impulse of the Holy Spirit and in light of their reading of the Scriptures in their own languages as well as insights they had received from the reformers, some groups expressed a new desire to follow in the footsteps of Jesus of Nazareth. They called for a "radical" reformation—that is, a movement that would go all the way to the root, and whose scope would be practical as well as doctrinal. They also called for a radical spirituality and ecclesiology, along with an authentic discipleship lived out within a community of faith.

Under the influence of this spirit, the Anabaptist movement emerged with the first adult baptisms on January 21, 1525. The movement was called "Anabaptist" (re-baptizers) by its adversaries because of its insistence on "believer's baptism" — a baptism free from the control of the ecclesiastical and political authorities. This commitment to believer's baptism set them apart from the rest of Christendom where infant baptism was the established practice, a practice associated in the minds of the poor with the tax burden of baptismal fees.

This Anabaptist movement was the central element of what came to be called the Radical Reformation, a faithful minority movement within the larger Reformation. It was a popular movement largely composed of common people — peasants, artisans, women — committed to life in community and patterned on the church of the first century, which they discovered in their reading of the New Testament. This model of the church was self-propagating, self-governing and self-sustaining, free from state and clerical control, and committed to the practice of justice, peace, and non-violence.

For the Anabaptists, spiritual authority did not rest with the Pope, nor with their theological professors, nor, for that matter, with their own congregational leaders. They found their source of authority in the gospel of Jesus in the Scriptures, which they read under the inspiration of the Spirit and interpreted within the community of faith. Rather than envisioning the church as a hierarchy, they viewed the congregation horizontally as an egalitarian community of sisters and brothers in Christ, independent from the state. Instead, they saw themselves as a voluntary fellowship made up of committed disciples baptized into a community of believers, whose pastors functioned not as authorities but as servants, using their gifts for the mutual well-being of the body rather than functioning as its authorities. In these communities Luther's vision of the priesthood of all believers became a visible reality.

This ecclesiological vision was so closely associated with radical implications for the political, social and cultural contexts of the period, and so subversive—among other reasons, for its "preferential option for the poor"—that some historians have called the early Anabaptists the "Revolutionaries of the Sixteenth Century," or the "Bolsheviks of the Sixteenth Century," or the "Left Wing of the Reformation."

Menno Simons (1496-1561), a Dutch ex-priest, was an early leader of this movement. Menno became one of the most articulate and influential leaders among the radical reformers in the Low Countries. In contrast to the Magisterial reformers of the time, Menno did not stand out so much as a theologian as he did for the pastoral care he provided to a fragmented minority movement in dire need of trusted and sacrificial leadership. Thanks to his pastoral leadership a network of base communities emerged, whose members came to be known popularly as the "Mennonites." These Mennonite communities were characterized by the kind of alternative and committed spirituality that Menno articulated in a truly notable passage in his writings:

> True evangelical faith is of such a nature that it cannot lie dormant, but manifests itself in all righteousness and works of love. . . . It clothes the naked; it feeds the hungry; it comforts the sorrowful; it shelters the destitute; it aids and consoles the sad; it returns good for evil; it serves those that harm it; it prays for those that persecute it; it teaches, admonishes, and reproves with the Word of the Lord; it seeks that which is lost; it binds up that which is wounded;

it heals that which is diseased and it saves that which is sound; it has become all things to all men.[1]

Catholic and Protestant authorities alike mercilessly persecuted, exiled, tortured and killed these Anabaptist "Mennonites." In their inter-church relationships both the established Catholic and Protestant churches largely ignored the mutual love which Jesus had taught his followers. The courageous cry for liberation of this faithful minority movement was met by rigidity, intolerance, prejudice and abuse that found physical, psychological, spiritual, personal and social expression. During the first twenty-five years of the movement, more than 2,500 Anabaptists suffered martyrdom. This represented roughly half of the total number of martyrs produced by religious persecution in Europe during the sixteenth century.

This large-scale persecution suffered by Anabaptist-Mennonite communities in Europe may well have been one cause for the social withdrawal that led, with the passage of time, to a posture of social sectarianism among some descendent groups. But at the same time, the experience has also led these communities to transform their suffering into one of the principal characteristics by which Anabaptist-Mennonites have come to be known during their five centuries of witness: as peace-makers, committed to nonviolence and to a radical sense of community, who seek to share Christ's love and to promote well-being, liberty, truth, justice and peace in every level of human relationships — personal, ecclesial, national and international. In so doing they have simply been reflecting the vision of Jesus: "Blessed are those who hunger and thirst for righteousness. . . . Blessed are those who are persecuted for righteousness' sake. . . . Blessed are the peacemakers for they will be called the children of God" (Mt. 5:6a,10a, 9).

The contribution of missionaries from the United States and Canada who, beginning in 1919, opened the way for the development of Anabaptist-Mennonite churches in Latin America will be remembered with appreciation. However, the Mennonite tradition which arrived from the North had lost, to a considerable degree, the radical characteristics of historic European Anabaptism. For many, being Mennonite in the United States and Canada implied a strong element of ethnic and cultural identity and a lesser degree of radical spiritual, pastoral, missional and theological distinction. It was only following World War II that a more truly Anabaptist identity began to emerge slowly among the Mennonites of the United States and Canada.

According to the latest statistics (2011), there are now more than 1,600,000 Anabaptist-Mennonite Christians in the world, scattered among 83 nations on 6 continents. Lamentably, among many of these groups—perhaps even the majority—Christian peacemaking, though affirmed in theory as a core conviction, is almost absent in practice. In the face of the overwhelming necessity of helping to construct a culture of peace in the world, many Anabaptist-Mennonite congregations have regrettably all but lost this dimension of their foundational identity and are neither pacifists nor active peacemakers within their wider contexts. Oriented by a hermeneutic that is too often shaped by Fundamentalism and insensitive to human need, they have become enclosed within themselves, trapped within their interconfessional prejudices and long-standing unresolved interpersonal conflicts. Many are therefore rendered powerless in the face of the call to be humanizing agents in preventing violence or participating in the peaceful transformation of conflicts within families, congregations and society at large.

In spite of this, however, a growing number of Anabaptist-Mennonites around the world remain open to restoring ecumenical relationships and are actively involved in the recovery of the original Anabaptist-Mennonite identity. These sisters and brothers in Christ are convinced that new possibilities of inter-church, inter-denominational, inter-confessional, and even inter-religious relationships are opening up with those around them, providing new opportunities for embodying and sharing a spirituality that is both radically Christian and genuinely Anabaptist.

By the grace of God, these relationships of "ecumenically minded" Anabaptist-Mennonites with other Protestants and Catholics are characterized by unity within diversity, by mutual respect, cooperation and enrichment. Making peace in these circles becomes a priority in the life and mission of their communities of faith. The initiatives taken by Mennonite World Conference and Mennonite Central Committee are examples of this openness. *Justapaz*, through its work in support of justice, peace and nonviolent action on the part of the Mennonite churches in Colombia is another powerful example. This same attitude was also demonstrated in a remarkable way by the World Council of Churches in its adoption of a proposal put forward by a German Mennonite, Fernando Ens. In 1999 Ens, representing the Association of Mennonite Churches of Germany, proposed that the first ten years of the twenty-first century (2001-2010) be designated as a "Decade to Overcome Violence," thereby shaping its ecumenical agenda throughout the world. This attitude also found expression in the quality of personal relationships characteristic of those Anabaptist-Mennonite communities whose identity—expressed in their daily lives—does not consist so much in institutional programs and projects as it does in simply "cultivating relationships of love: with God, among themselves, with their neighbors, and with their environment."[2]

This radical ecclesiology that our sixteenth century Anabaptist ancestors have bequeathed to us as a spiritual legacy has sometimes been cut off and diminished, or even exchanged for ecclesiologies that seem to be more functional, more fully in accord with the status quo, or better aligned with the

Life Together in the Spirit

expectations of the institutional church. However, whenever a faithful minority movement—whatever its denominational origins—commits itself to incarnate a radical new identity as inclusive communities of human solidarity, of justice and of peace in following Jesus of Nazareth, the kingdom of God will be evident in all of its life-giving power.

– Guillermo C. Font[3]

1. *The Complete Writings of Menno Simons*, trans. Leonard Verduin and ed. John C. Wenger (Scottdale, Pa.: Herald Press, 1956), 307.

2. For the past ten years this is the motto has expressed the spiritual commitment and peacemaking vocation of the *Iglesia Evangélica Menonita de Trenque Lauquen,* the second oldest Spanish-speaking congregation in the world (founded in 1920).

3. Guillermo Font is director and editor of *Ediciones Kairós* and pastoral counselor of the Evangelical Mennonite Church in Trenque Lauquen, Argentina.

Introduction

During the final decades of the twentieth century and the early years of the twenty-first, the theme of Christian spirituality has once again come to occupy an important place in Protestant thought. This has not always been the case.

As Protestants we had only heard of Catholic forms of spirituality whose principal practitioners included the Trappist monks—known for the austerity of their lifestyle and their vows of perpetual silence—the cloistered nuns, or some of the other contemplative Catholic orders. With the general Protestant rejection of the Catholic orders that accompanied the sixteenth-century Reformation, we have generally underestimated, if not totally rejected, these and other similar expressions of Christian spirituality.

Instead, we have used terms like "devotional life" to refer to those attitudes and activities that nurture the inner dimensions of faith deep within our souls. We have tended to understand "spirituality" as a sort of inner, invisible energy that sustains and supports our lives as Christians in the world.

Not only has Protestant thought been dominated by this inward and highly abstract concept of spirituality; it has also tended to become almost exclusively individual and

1

essentially private. Even our congregational spirituality—
expressed in practices like common prayer, Bible study
and worship—has generally been directed toward the
personal edification of individual members, rather than an
integration of practices into a shared missional fellowship
characteristic of an authentic community of faith.

The spirituality of the first disciples of Jesus, however,
seems to have included all aspects of their life. In order to
fully understand a spirituality that is truly biblical, we will
need to overcome the false dichotomies we use to divide
ourselves: that is, the spiritual, inner, and other-worldly
from the part of us that is material, outer, and worldly.
Christian spirituality does not consist of a life of
contemplation *instead of* action, nor of withdrawal *instead of*
full participation in the social order. Rather, Christian
spirituality is the experience of every dimension of human
life being oriented around and animated by the very Spirit
of Jesus.

For this reason, we dedicate the first two chapters of this
little book to a review of Christian spirituality during the
first century. There we discover a holistic spirituality that
consisted of following Jesus, under the impulse of his
Spirit and in the context of a Messianic community
radically living out their faith together. It was a spirituality
deeply rooted in God's grace, nourished and shared in the
common life of the community of faith, and incarnated
fully in its participation in God's mission in the world.

The third and fourth chapters describe the essential
characteristics of Anabaptist spirituality in the sixteenth

century. The Anabaptist movement was only one of many movements of radical renewal that have arisen throughout the church's history. Oriented by a commitment to Jesus and the example of the primitive Christian community of the first century, these movements have recovered to a remarkable degree—in their own life and within their own historical contexts—a spirituality amazingly similar to that of the Christian communities of the first century. In addition to the Anabaptists, a list of those movements could include groups like the Waldensians and the Franciscans of the twelfth and thirteenth centuries, the seventeenth century Quakers, the classic Pentecostal movement of the early twentieth century, the base ecclesial communities within Latin American Catholicism of the past generation, and many more.

Finally, this brief study of radical spirituality concludes with a series of reflections on the possibilities for interchurch dialogue among the variety of spiritualities in the twenty-first century—reflecting a range of visions, convictions and lifestyles—but especially between the present day heirs of historic Anabaptism and other traditions. We have the obligation to engage continually in fraternal ecumenical dialogue with Christians from other traditions. We reject as false the idea that apostasy and heresy are permanent or hereditary. Likewise, we reject the idea that authentic faith is automatically passed on from one generation to another. For that reason, our churches must always remain in dialogue with Christians whose history has been different than ours, and who have other ways of thinking and acting, even if their spiritual ancestors in others times and contexts may have persecuted our spiritual forebearers for honestly held differences.

Christian Spirituality in the First Century
Part I

As already noted in the introduction, the spirituality of Jesus' disciples touched every dimension of their lives. The biblical terms "flesh" or "carnal" and "spirit" or "spiritual" do not refer to two separate dimensions of human life — one outer and the other inner — but rather to two different ways of living, two orientations, two lifestyles. To be "spiritual" is to live every aspect of our lives inspired by and aligned with the Spirit of Christ. To be "carnal" is to be oriented by a very different spirit.

The community of faith in which Mother Theresa of Calcutta participated offers an example of this kind of spirituality. For her, "touching the untouchables" meant to "touch the body of Christ." To love in this utterly unselfish way was a form of prayer. One does not stop praying in order to serve; neither does one stop serving in order to pray. Authentic spirituality is "all pervasive."[1] This is the same vision we find reflected in Matthew 25, where the nations will be judged according to how they responded to the needs of the hungry, the resident aliens (that is, the undocumented immigrants in their midst), the poor, the sick, the imprisoned, and the outcasts in their land. To the surprise of all, Jesus reminded his hearers by saying "just as you did it to the least of these who are members of my family, you did it to me" (Mt. 25:40).

RECOVERING THE ESSENCE OF CHRISTIAN SPIRITUALITY

The cross of Jesus offers us the clearest model of an authentically Christian spirituality, reflected in the teachings of the New Testament. The cross is both a sign of complete identification with God and of total solidarity with the world. The cross reflects with absolute clarity the spirit of Jesus as well as the spirituality that his disciples would be called to imitate.

In this sense, the cross is the most eloquent intercessory prayer to the Father on behalf of the world. At the same time, it is the most energetic and convincing response of God to the powers of evil. Therefore, in the cross of Jesus— as well as in the cross that his followers are called to assume—we find the very essence of Christian spirituality.

Christian spirituality is the process of following Jesus Christ, animated by His Spirit, in the context of a truly radical (i.e., Christ-rooted) fellowship of faith experienced within the Body of Christ. This process leads into an ever-growing solidarity with Christ, in which Christians identify themselves fully with the life and death of Jesus. For followers of Jesus, the primary symbol of this living, dying and rising again is baptism, by which we are initiated into a truly Christian spirituality (Rom. 6:4). This spirituality is marked by our following the Jesus of history within our own historical contexts. It is by the power of the living Spirit of Jesus himself, freely given to his followers, that this radical spirituality becomes a possibility.

It is a spirituality of the road.

BIBLICAL CHARACTERISTICS OF CHRISTIAN SPIRITUALITY

The New Testament offers the following descriptions of spirituality which provide guidelines for assessing the authenticity of any particular Christian spirituality.[2]

1. *A truly Christian spirituality is based on the divine initiative of God's promise.* The God of the Bible is the God who promises to save His people, freeing them from the powers of evil. No single historic expression of God's saving intervention on behalf of His people completely exhausts this divine promise. With thankful hearts we embrace every sign and symbol of God's transforming grace within human history that points in the direction of the kingdom of God. However, for Christians, these historic expressions are always provisional. With Jesus, we continue to pray for the coming of God's Kingdom in all of its fullness. Our commitment to follow Jesus must always be in anticipation of God's Kingdom still to come in all of its saving glory.

2. *This spirituality is an expression of hope.* It consists of believing that which sometimes seem to be impossible: namely, the reconciliation of humans among themselves and with God in a truly radical fellowship characterized by justice and peace. For this reason, joy is one of the principal characteristics of the messianic community — the

community that trusts more in the power of God than in its own possibilities. This joyful hope fills followers of Jesus with the confidence and security that they need to live out the distinctive values of God's reign against the current of our culture. Within the economy of God's Kingdom no effort that is aligned with God's rule of justice and peace will be lost (Heb. 1:11ff.; Rom. 5:4ff.).

3. *A truly evangelical spirituality implies solidarity with the suffering, death and resurrection of Jesus.* Just as Jesus lived and died—"the just for the unjust"—so also the salvation of the oppressors will come about through the nonviolent actions and suffering of the oppressed on behalf of the oppressor. It has been the experience of the messianic community that its salvation comes alone through the vicarious suffering of Jesus. Therefore, we confess freely that although the suffering, death and resurrection of Jesus are truly unique in their saving power, they are not Christ's alone. In our innocent suffering on behalf of others we are "completing what is lacking in Christ's afflictions for the sake of his body" (Col. 1:24).

4. *According to the New Testament, the purpose of the saving work of Christ is the restoration of communion among a humanity alienated from God and from each other.* The restoration of fraternal relationships within the family of God requires the transformation of self-centered men and women into brothers and sisters shaped by a radically new fellowship of love. We experience this communion when we share our possessions for each other's well-being or when true authority is expressed in the form of mutual

service (Mt. 20:25-28; Acts 2:43-45; 4:32-35). The example of Jesus, as well as that of the early Christian community, reminds us that authentic communion is characterized by a radically new understanding of the exercise of power, both in socio-political relationships and economic interactions.

5. *All spirituality that is authentically Christian will be characterized by this radical fellowship of love.* At stake here is not merely avoiding anything that might harm our neighbor, but rather actively pursuing our neighbor's well-being. To love as God has loved us in Jesus Christ is to offer our life itself for the neighbor in very concrete ways (1 Jn. 3:16-17). The love of God, of which the New Testament speaks, is much more than merely God's love directed to us. It is also bigger than the love that we should have for God. At its deepest level, it is to love as God loves—that is, a willingness to lay down our lives for the neighbor in acts of unselfish heroism, as well as in the long process of yielding ourselves and our interests to the well-being of others in ordinary daily relationships.

A SPIRITUALITY DEEPLY ROOTED IN THE GOD OF GRACE

A truly Christian spirituality is rooted deeply in the God of grace who has been most fully revealed in Jesus Christ. It is though the Jesus of history and his Spirit, that we can best know the Father, for Jesus "is the image of the invisible God" (Col 1:15). Instead of speculating about the divinity of Jesus—based on the attributes systematic theologians have traditionally assigned to God—would it not be better to proceed just as the church in the first century did? They caught a vision of the invisible God before their very eyes in the person of Jesus and in the life he lived.

The God of authentic Christian spirituality has taken the initiative in our liberation from the powers of evil. God has first loved us! In reality, this has always been God's way of acting. The people of God were freed from slavery in Egypt, thanks to God's merciful initiative. Classical Protestantism has sometimes asserted that the Old Testament is characterized by the law and a righteousness of works, while the New Testament is characterized by grace and the good news of the gospel. But in reality, Israel was redeemed out of Egypt by grace and the people of the New Covenant are invited to live according to "the law of Christ."

It has always been God's intention to form a people in His image, a people that bears His name. Jesus not only teaches the character of God; he is also the perfect image of what God has always intended humanity to be. This divine project, which points toward the restoration of all creation to its original purpose, will culminate in the restoration of God's reign of justice and peace in every aspect of life. An authentic Christian spirituality is in complete harmony with this divine purpose and participates fully in its saving process.

As we know, the powers of evil and the dominant values of the fallen world conspire to distort the true image of God revealed by Jesus. We are prone to create idols that take the place of God. These idols lay claim to our loyalties, and we dedicate our time and our energies to them. But the God of Abraham, of Moses and of the prophets is a God who is active in human history, liberating His people from these false gods and the false loyalties that enslave us. In this, God was at work especially in the Messiah, who is the culmination of the process of this progressive revelation: "No one can know . . . the Father except by the Son and anyone to whom the Son chooses to reveal him" (Lk. 10:22). This is a God who is truly different. Only a genuinely authentic Christian spirituality will be able to experience God fully and to show God's good news to others without twisting or distorting the message.

A SPIRITUALITY OF FOLLOWING JESUS

Since God has revealed Himself uniquely and fully in Jesus, the only way to know Him is by following Jesus Christ (Heb. 1:1-3). Hans Denck, a radical reformer of the sixteenth century said, "No one can truly know Christ unless he follow him in his life,"[3] a conviction that the heirs of the Anabaptist movement continue to hold. Therefore, following Jesus concretely is, without doubt, the most fundamental element of a truly authentic Christian spirituality.

Segundo Galilea, a leading Chilean theologian of the past generation, has expressed it this way:

> The originality and the authenticity of Christian spirituality consists in following a God who has taken on our human condition; who had a history like ours; who has lived our experiences, who made choices; who dedicated himself to a cause for which he had to suffer; who experienced successes, joys and failures; and who yielded his life. This man, Jesus of Nazareth, is like us in every way except that he was without sin. In Jesus, all the fullness of God dwelt; so he is the only model for our life, as humans and as Christians.[4]

Lamentably, Christians have not traditionally thought about spirituality in these terms. Catholic spirituality, as well as that of classical Protestantism, has generally thought of the divine nature of Jesus as the Final Judge to be worshipped or as a propitiatory sacrifice for the appeasement of divine wrath—but only rarely as a Lord to be followed in daily life. This has contributed to the emergence of a highly inward, abstract, and other-worldly spirituality.

Yet according to the vision of the New Testament, the words, deeds, ideals and commandments of Jesus of Nazareth offer the only path to a knowledge of God (Jn. 14:5-11). Jesus has revealed the true nature of God to us— all-powerful precisely in His longsuffering love and compassion. In Jesus we discover the qualities of God's reign and the model for our lives. This is not a legalistic or slavish imitation—wearing sandals, for example, or working as a carpenter, or remaining celibate—but rather following him by adopting his attitudes, his Spirit, his values, and his way of being and actions in the world. True Christian spirituality will focus especially on the manner in which we embrace the attitudes, the Spirit, the deeds and words of Jesus in the concrete expressions of discipleship in daily life.

One of the best summaries we have of a spirituality that reflects the reign of God, inaugurated by Jesus, is found in the Beatitudes as recorded in Matthew 5. As a synthesis of the entire Sermon on the Mount, the Beatitudes capture the qualities that Jesus taught and modeled. Unfortunately, in the centuries following Christ's death and resurrection, the church has tended to assign a utopian character to the teachings of the Sermon on the Mount so that they came to be understood as "counsels of perfection," appropriate only for a small minority, like those in religious orders, who take the Christian life extremely seriously.

The primitive church of the first century, however, used the Beatitudes to instruct new disciples. They clearly must have expected that these qualities would characterize the lives of all believers. And the way in which the Beatitudes summarize the spirituality reflected throughout the entire New Testament indicates that they were never intended as unrealistic ideals.

To be sure, the Beatitudes are truly prophetic in their character. As such, there will always be tension between the spirituality that they reflect and the level of understanding and practice achieved in the Christian community. We need to be honest—these values clash with our human inclinations. There is an element of scandal in the Gospel with its understandings of mercy and forgiveness, nonviolence, sexual chastity, and spiritual poverty. This should not surprise us because these are the values that characterize the kingdom of God, and they are possible only thanks to the empowerment of the Holy Spirit.

The Beatitudes summarize the blessedness of life under God's rule. Foundational for the spirituality of the Messianic community, they presuppose a shared life within the community of God's reign rather than heroic efforts to live them out as solitary individuals. The spirituality of the Beatitudes is "good news" in the fundamental sense of the word *evangelium*—the full-orbed good news of social, political and economic well-being. The eight beatitudes listed in Matthew 5 are therefore not merely isolated spiritual virtues offered to disciples of Jesus as options to be chosen or disregarded according to personal preferences. Rather, they describe a truly Messianic spirituality in a global sense. All of them, taken together, describe a fully integrated spirituality that characterizes life under the reign of God.

1. "Blessed are the poor in Spirit . . ."

A posture of spiritual poverty is fundamental to all Christian spirituality. Spiritual poverty consists of freely assuming the spiritual condition of being a child in the family of the Father. It is both the attitude and the practice of absolute dependence on God, trusting in God's providence as well as God's protection. It is that intimate relationship of utter confidence in God that Jesus himself demonstrated so clearly when he dared to call God, *Abba,* and taught his disciples to do the same.

But the Gospels do not permit an abstract or spiritualized understanding of this poverty. Sharing life together in the new community of the Messiah and living in radical dependence on God's providence cuts off all of our idolatrous and materialistic attitudes and practices at their very roots. "Choosing to be poor" (as the translation of the *Nueva Biblia Española* reads) in a world oriented in the opposite direction implies a solidarity with Jesus— with the spirit and practice of poverty that he assumed freely and concretely in his mission in the world.

2. *"Blessed are those who mourn . . ."*

Living out the values of God's reign in the midst of the world necessarily assumes solidarity with human suffering. It involves living in *sympathy* (literally, "to suffer together with") with those who suffer—indeed, freely assuming suffering on behalf of others. This innocent and vicarious suffering is absolutely central to an authentic Christian spirituality.

The Old Testament prophets spoke of the saving virtue that is found in innocent suffering freely assumed on behalf of others. But in Jesus we encounter the fullest expression of this reality. Our identification with Christ and our solidarity with fellow humans who suffer from all the various consequences of evil in the world calls us to take up the cross, even on behalf of our oppressors, with the full confidence that the resurrection of Jesus Christ imparts to us—namely, that our innocent and vicarious suffering will not be lost in God's salvific plan to restore creation.

3. *"Blessed are the meek . . ."*

The meekness of the third beatitude is intimately related to the poverty of spirit noted in the first beatitude. It includes the inner fortitude that enables us to steadfastly resist the pressures of sin without yielding to its claims. It is the capacity to resist evil tenaciously without doing violence to the evildoer. This kind of meekness is rooted solidly on our hope and confidence in God. The meek person is one who truly believes that evil can be overcome with good. It calls us to reject the temptation to avenge ourselves with any form of violence or retaliation—to renounce all violence in the quest for justice and to struggle against evil with "clean hands" and a "pure heart." Far from being an ineffective strategy, this is, in fact, the strategy of the cross, uniquely and powerfully incarnated by Jesus of Nazareth.

4. *"Blessed are those who hunger and thirst for righteousness..."*

Biblical justice consists of healthy relationships with God and with our fellow human beings in the context of a community that is absolutely dependant on the saving actions of God, both for its life together and for its very survival. Biblical justice includes the full range of interpersonal relationships, and is anchored in the faithfulness of God reflected in the common life of the human community that bears His name. This justice is visible only in the context of God's righteous (or just) reign.

Biblical justice, in contrast with what is generally called retributive justice, consists in giving people what they *need* rather than what they may *deserve*, be that reward or punishment. For this reason, we read over and over again in Scripture about God's justice for the widows and the orphans, for the stranger in the land, and for the poor and the oppressed. Authentic Christian spirituality expresses itself through our participation in the saving activity of God that leads to the restoration of just relationships among humans. It is within this community of salvation that the "hunger and thirst for righteousness"—just relationships among all—will be satisfied.

5. "Blessed are the merciful . . ."

It is in showing mercy that we become most like God. The story of the Good Samaritan provides us with a clear and concrete example of a spirituality characterized by mercy. To the degree that we are able to show mercy we will be in a condition to receive God's mercy for ourselves.

Mercy in the Gospels means, first of all, to forgive wholeheartedly in the same way as God forgives us (Mt. 18:35). In the second place, to be merciful is to unselfishly come to the aid of the afflicted and the needy. The limits of this mercy are not found in the one who extends acts of mercy, but in the capacity of the "neighbor" to receive mercy. What Jesus has taught us about the nature of mercy simply underscores the fact that a true Christian spirituality is characterized by our willingness to freely heap forgiveness upon our adversaries and to share lavishly with the needy.

6. Blessed are the pure in heart . . ."

The "purity of heart" evident in all authentic Christian spirituality can probably be best understood in light of Psalm 24:3-5a:

> Who shall ascend the hill of the Lord? . . . Those who have clean hands and pure hearts, who do not lift up their souls to what is false, and do not swear deceitfully. They will receive blessing from the Lord.

This purity of heart expresses itself in acts of integrity and in relationships characterized by faithfulness. Biblical spirituality is characterized by a close relationship between our inner attitudes ("purity of heart") and our external practices ("clean hands"). To know and to experience God is to obey and accompany God in His salvific actions, without divided loyalties.

7. "Blessed are the peacemakers . . ."

Those who work for peace are children of God, especially in the sense that in doing so they are like their Father who is the Peacemaker, par excellence. The God of the Bible does not rest in His efforts to restore wholeness, or Shalom, to all areas of brokenness in creation. Jesus was fully committed to the restoration of peace—reconciliation with enemies occupied his attention throughout his lifetime as well as in his death. Activities oriented toward the restoration of Shalom will characterize all authentically Christian spiritualties.

8. "Blessed are those who are persecuted for righteousness sake..."

The Beatitudes find their summation in the innocent suffering of God's people. The spirituality that they reflect was countercultural, then as well as now. Persecution for faithfulness to God's reign of justice and peace was the lot of the prophets, it marked the fate of Jesus, and it continues to characterize the community faithful to its Messianic calling. Biblically speaking, witness and martyrdom go hand in hand (*marturía* is the Greek word for witness). When we remember that there have been more martyrs in our lifetime than in any other period of Christian history we recognize the contemporary relevance of the Beatitudes and their importance for our understanding and practice of authentic spirituality. This is true for the entire church, not merely for the church in the global south. The powers of death — arrayed as they are against God and His intention for the restoration of justice, peace, salvation, and life in our world — remind us that the spirituality of God's people is inherently countercultural.

The spirituality of the Beatitudes is not an unattainable ideal, but rather a realistic and visible reflection of the Spirit — the words and the deeds of Jesus of Nazareth. The Beatitudes express the central values that characterized the life of the messianic community of the first century.

To follow Jesus is not a purely spiritual matter in the sense of being an inner or invisible reality in the life of the disciple. Rather, discipleship is a visible and concrete reality that expresses itself through the attitudes and actions described in the Beatitudes.

Christian Spirituality in the First Century
Part II

A SPIRITUALITY ROOTED IN THE SPIRIT OF JESUS

Following his death and resurrection, Jesus bestowed his spirit upon his followers. Since that time Jesus Christ continues to be present in his Body, through the presence of his spirit. The Holy Spirit, present in the church, is the same spirit with which Jesus was anointed for his Messianic mission. For that reason, Christian spirituality does not consist only of following Jesus (who is the Way), but also of sharing the life of Jesus (who is the Life), empowered by the presence of his living spirit. Thus, a truly authentic Christian spirituality is Trinitarian—a life lived in absolute dependence on the Father, oriented by its commitment to follow Jesus, whose life together is permeated by the Holy Spirit.

The Old Testament presents the spirit of God as the source of life as well as the one who sustains the life of God's people. The New Testament describes the activity of the Spirit in the context of the creation of new life and the ongoing sustenance of that life.

Likewise, the Gospel of John presents Jesus Christ as the fulfillment of Judaism and the Jewish institutions that sustained the religious and social status quo of the period. Participation in the reign of God, now restored by the

Messiah, called for the transformation of Pharisaic spirituality—the best that first-century Judaism had to offer. As Jesus explained to Nicodemus, being transformed by the spirit of Christ required that one be "born again from above." The creation of a new humanity transformed by the Spirit of God was an essential element in the prophetic vision of the coming Messianic era (Ez. 36:25-28). Thanks to the spirit that Jesus bestowed upon his followers, the life that would correspond to the new era (i.e., "eternal life") now became a possibility.

That same spirit—the presence of the living Christ—continues to sustain the common life of God's people. One of the principal functions of the Spirit is to make clear the teachings of Jesus in the faith community in order to facilitate obedience in discipleship (Jn. 14:26). The Holy Spirit also inspires the gift of prophecy within the community for discerning the paths that faithful living will take (Jn. 16:13). And in a very special way, the Spirit enables the church to witness (*marturía*) with faithfulness to God's reign. For its task of continuing faithfully the witness of Jesus in the world, the Spirit encourages and strengthens the Church in its witness of suffering and martyrdom (Jn. 15:26-27; 16:1-4; cf. Mt. 10:10; Mk. 13:10; Lk. 12:11-12; 21:12-15).

Thus, the saving presence of Jesus Christ is continued in the world by the Holy Spirit acting through the church. The work of the Spirit embraces the entire spectrum of Christ's saving work. It includes the creation of a community of faith that bears the image of its Creator. It includes the Spirit's impulse to faithfully obey the teachings of Jesus. It empowers the followers of Jesus in their witness in the world, including suffering for the cause of God's Kingdom. And it guides the church to glorify Christ through its experiences as a reconciled and reconciling community.

Scattered throughout the epistles, we find a series of phrases that reflect the New Testament understanding of authentic Christian spirituality: "to walk according to the Spirit;" "to be led by the Spirit;" "to live according to the Spirit;" "to set the mind on the Spirit;" "to receive the Spirit;" "to have the first fruits of the Spirit;" "to be guided by the Spirit;" "to sow to the Spirit;" "to reap eternal life from the Spirit," etc.[5]

To live according to the spirit of Christ is to take Jesus seriously as the model for our lives and actions. The Spirit, who is the impulse and the inspiration for our spirituality, is the spirit of Jesus. Although this is the opposite of living according to the flesh, in Paul's thought "spirit" and "flesh" are not two mutually contradictory human characteristics. Rather, they refer to two opposing spheres of human existence. One is the sphere in which human life is oriented by the spirit of Jesus; the other sphere is a life opposed to God's restorative and salvific purpose.

Galatians 5:19-23 offers two lists of human characteristics that describe the fundamental differences separating the sphere of the spirit from that of the flesh. The lists are representative of a whole series of similar contrasts that we find scattered throughout Paul's writings (e.g., Col. 3:5-15; Eph. 4:2-3; I Cor. 6:9-11; II Cor. 6:4-6). The vices included in these lists probably reflect the areas in which the church's conflict with the values and lifestyle of Greco-Roman society in the first century was most intense. On the other hand, the virtues listed here—or fruits of the Spirit—were characteristics of Jesus, as he had lived among them: love, joy, peace, patience, kindness, generosity, faithfulness, gentleness and self-control (Gal. 5:22-23). They saw these things in Jesus as they had never experienced before. These virtues are held up as models for creating and strengthening a truly authentic Christian spirituality.

In all probability these lists were used for the instruction of new believers who were coming into the communities of the early church. Each of these virtues represents a concrete expression of the spirituality of the first-century communities. They reflect the firm conviction shared in the early church that the lifestyle and values of the Kingdom inaugurated by the Messiah would continue to characterize the community of faith under the impulse of the spirit of the risen Lord. Those who instructed new catechumens to follow Jesus in the way of his kingdom continually accompanied these new converts, walking with them in the presence of Christ's Spirit.

"To walk in the Spirit" meant to continue the life of the Kingdom that Jesus had proclaimed in this new community of the Spirit. Jesus himself was the clearest model of what life in the new community was about. In him, the early church saw the fullest example of the fruits of the Spirit. And, as they understood it, the most crucial role of the Spirit was to inspire this ongoing fruit-bearing spirituality within the Body of Christ.

A SPIRITUALITY NOURISHED AND SHARED WITHIN THE COMMUNITY OF FAITH

Christian spirituality is, by its very nature, experienced in community. The Spirit is present and active primarily in and through the Body of Christ, the church. Spiritualities that are completely individualistic and private lack biblical authenticity and will surely fail. Sooner or later they are destined to become mere ideologies or ethical systems. But a spirituality that is truly Christian—expressed in life together inspired by the spirit of Christ—will be nourished in the church, which is a community of the Spirit.

According to the New Testament, holiness is essentially a *corporate* experience—saintliness is communal. The Bible does not recognize the concept of solitary sainthood or a purity focused strictly on the individual. When the Scriptures do speak of saints, almost without exception the term is used in its plural form. Indeed, the expression "the saints" is usually a synonym for "the church." Only within the communion of God's people is it possible to be "holy as God is holy" (I Pet. 1:16).

The individualism that dominates the thought and vocabulary of the modern Western world has distorted the way we view the lives of those exemplary men and women of God in the history of the church. Instead of being the lonely spiritual giants that we often imagine, the saints were men and women who participated fully in the life and mission of God's people in the world. Their spirituality was nurtured by the same sources that God provides for all followers of Jesus through communion within the Body of Christ.

Therefore, Jesus can be followed authentically only in the company of other followers of Jesus. To follow Jesus is to walk together with our sisters and brothers in "The Way." This was one of the primary images the early Christians used to understand and communicate their corporate identity. The book of Acts refers to the Messianic community as "The Way" at least nine times (9:2; 16:17; 18:26; 19:9, 23; 22:4; 24:14. 22). When we add to this the many occasions where the Gospels and the Epistles use this same metaphor to refer to the relationship of Jesus with his followers, we are confronted with an image of fundamental importance for understanding the essential nature of the church.

It would not be an exaggeration to say that the spirituality of God's people is fundamentally a "spirituality of the Way." Indeed, the image of "exodus" or "way" (*exhodos/hodos* in Greek) plays a major role in the biblical understanding of salvation history in both the Old and the New Testaments.

Thus, the call of Abraham reported in Genesis 12 was, in a concrete sense, to participate in an "exodus"—that is, an invitation to follow Yahweh in His way. More than merely a geographical relocation, it called for a radically new spirituality. "I have chosen him, that he may charge his children and his household after him to keep the way of the Lord by doing righteousness and justice" (Gen. 18:19).

The liberation of Israel from Egyptian slavery was also an exodus, both in the literal sense but also in a metaphorical sense. With a "strong arm" Yahweh redeemed his people, liberating them from their slavery in Egypt. But he also liberated them from Egypt itself and the imperial system it represented. Ultimately, the conflict was between Yahweh, the God of the oppressed, and Pharaoh, the lord of Egypt and the incarnation of its god. The newness of life for which Israel was liberated from Egypt was figuratively and literally a new spirituality of "The Way."

Subsequently, the prophet would see Israel's return from exile as yet another exodus (Is. 40:1-11) in which the first exodus would serve as a paradigm for Yahweh's new redemptive initiative. Once again, prisoners would be liberated and Yahweh would be merciful to the poor (Is. 49:8-13). Once again, God's redeeming action would consist in the restoration of an authentic spirituality of the Way.

References to the historical exodus abound in the Gospels, which repeatedly describe the Messianic restoration as a new exodus. Thus, the New Testament presents Jesus as the "new Moses" who gives a "new law" from God on a "new mountain" to orient the spirituality of a "new people" of God (Mt. 5-7). The gospels describe the death of Jesus, which was the culmination of an entire life dedicated to the liberation of an enslaved humanity, again in terms of a "new exodus" (Lk. 9:31). And, undoubtedly, the clearest metaphor used in the Gospels to describe the spirituality of this new Messianic Community is that of following Jesus in "the way."

For these reasons, the spirituality of the people of God throughout all of their history has been characterized as walking in the Way of God—the Way of liberation from all the enslaving powers of evil; the Way that not only leads to life, but is also the Way in which abundant life is already experienced now. It is in this Way that we know and walk with the God of our salvation (Dt. 8:2-6). The people of God, according to the biblical vision, are made up of "those of the Way." To know God, in the biblical sense, is to experience God in concrete human relationships. We know God as we follow obediently in God's Way. The spirituality of this people of "the Way" finds its source, its model and its dynamic in Jesus, the One we follow in "the Way."

A SPIRITUALITY INCARNATED IN GOD'S MISSION IN THE WORLD

The love of God for humanity has taken its clearest form in the mission of Jesus in the world. We have witnessed this love, not only in how Jesus lived but in the way in which he laid down his life for others, especially for the marginalized, the alienated and the enemies of God. In this same way God's love is to be incarnated in the community of faith (I Jn. 3:16-17). This is the way in which Paul imitated Christ (I Cor. 11:1; 4:16; Phil. 3:17); and it is precisely this same tangible model that we are called to follow as "imitators of God, as beloved children" (Eph. 5:1-2).

The spirituality of God's people is to be expressed in every aspect of their lives. God's people imitate God—that is, they follow Jesus and they live out the communion of the Spirit—in all dimensions of life, both personal and corporate. To be sure, the presence of the living Lord in the world is experienced most fully in the life and mission of the church. But authentic spirituality builds relationships not only within the community of faith; it is also the impulse and inspiration for the church's participation in God's mission in the world. The same spirituality that edifies the Body of Christ is also fundamental to its missional witness in the world.

The missional presence of Christ's Body in the world consists essentially in discipleship. Here again, Jesus is the model. Jesus' call to discipleship is an invitation to participate in the very same mission that God commended to His Messiah. To follow Jesus, who was "sent by the Father," is to share in the same vocation, characterized by the same spirituality, and by the same mission.

Matthew 10 briefly describes the mission of the apostles. Yet we should note that this was not a mission intended exclusively for the twelve disciples. In reality Matthew 10 reflects the missional spirituality that characterized the first-century community of the early church in which Matthew participated. Here we see that the whole life of Jesus—but in a very special way, his suffering and death—provided the ingredients for the spirituality of the

Matthean community: "A disciple is not above the teacher, nor a slave above the master" (Mt. 10:24).

To summarize: an authentically Christian spirituality is one that expresses itself in the mission of Christ. For that reason, it is a spirituality of the cross in the deepest sense: "Whoever does not take up his cross and follow me is not worthy of me. Those who find their life will lose it, and those who lose their life for my sake will find it" (Mt. 10: 38-39).

Spirituality in Sixteenth-Century Anabaptism
Part I

The Anabaptist movement of the sixteenth century inherited much of the monastic spiritual tradition of the Middle Ages, especially their dualistic understandings and practices in the area of church-world relationships. But the Anabaptists rejected the long standing liturgical-sacramental tradition as well as the hierarchical structures of the church and monastery. Instead, they promoted intensive Bible study in more spiritual family structures, in which their gatherings were held in their homes and their relationships were familial. They saw themselves as brothers and sisters. Here they developed a strong sense of a universal calling to Christian discipleship and mission, together with the exercise of the freedom of the will that this implied.

The Anabaptist vision was forged out of their experience of a fresh reading the Scriptures in the context of their communities of faith. Rather than emphasizing the highly contemplative life of meditation and prayer, common among the Catholic Orders, or focusing on right doctrine, as mainstream Protestants tended to do, Anabaptists asked, "How can we be obedient to the Gospel of Jesus Christ?"

Although medieval monasticism and Anabaptism held much in common, their different understandings of the Christian community, or the church, resulted in different spiritualities. Instead of an abstract or an other-worldly mysticism, the Anabaptists emphasized the practice of obedience, active love, and the integration of faith and works. Their focus was not so much on cultivating a common spiritual life through contemplation or other introspective practices, as it was practicing a life of prayer, peace, integrity and humility in the context of radical communal social relationships. Theirs was a Christ-centered quest to know and worship God. Moreover, the spirituality of the Anabaptists was a gift of grace bestowed by the Spirit, not the product of human effort.

Although the Anabaptist movement of the sixteenth century was clearly diverse, few groups expressed interest in solitary contemplation, introspection or ascetic practices as such. What did interest them was the prospect of "walking in newness of life," thanks to a regeneration experienced through the marvelous grace of God that expressed itself in the integration of faith *and* works, of the individual *and* the community, and of service *and* witness. The spirituality of the Anabaptists—especially among leaders such as Balthasar Hubmaier and Menno Simons who strongly emphasized the written Word—was essentially centered on their experience of the Holy Spirit.

A SPIRITUALITY INSPIRED BY THE SPIRIT OF CHRIST

All aspects of the Anabaptist movement were inspired by a profound understanding of the role of the Spirit in the life of the Church. They insisted that the Holy Spirit's work in human hearts was crucial both for beginning and for sustaining a life of faith. Many early Anabaptists, including Balthasar Hubmaier, who was one of the least "Pentecostal" among them, spoke of three baptisms—a baptism of the Spirit, of water and of blood (I Jn. 5:7-8).

The Spirit also played a fundamental and active role in all scriptural interpretation. In their biblical interpretations, the early Anabaptists were more "spiritual" and less literal than most of the other reform movements of the sixteenth century. Classical Protestantism placed much more emphasis on an objective, literal reading of the Scriptures, while the Anabaptists tended to give more importance to a subjective, inner, or spiritual, reading of the text.[6]

This insistence of simple unlearned persons on the powerful role of the Spirit in biblical interpretation was, in part at least, a protest against the monopoly of an established religion that restricted the interpretation of Scriptures to the church hierarchy and its clergy. In the Catholic tradition, clerical authority focused on the sacraments. Within classical Protestantism clerical authority resided in the power of their academic erudition.

Testimonies from Anabaptists in all regions where the movement took root, by contrast, unanimously agreed that it was impossible to understand the Scriptures fully without the baptism of the Spirit. For this reason, Lutherans often accused the Anabaptists of "spiritualistic antinomianism" or a "spiritualistic anarchy," following in the path of the Saxon radical, Thomas Müntzer.

The debate between Martin Luther and Thomas Müntzer—the radical reformer in Lutheran territories especially noted for his spiritualistic tendencies—clearly illustrates these two positions. Müntzer assigned a preparatory, or instructional, role to the Scriptures in "slaying" the believer so that he or she might awaken to the inner Word and respond to the Spirit. Without the Spirit within, Müntzer insisted, one "does not know how to say anything deeply about God, even if he had eaten through a hundred Bibles!"[7] To this Luther responded that "he would not trust Müntzer either, even if he had swallowed the Holy Ghost feathers and all."[8]

Thus, the Anabaptists did not identify the Word of God with the written scriptures in a simple and direct way. Instead, they insisted that the "inner word," the voice of God's Spirit, gave authority and value to the "outer word" of the written Scriptures. The Scriptures were important for knowing the will of God, but not absolutely indispensable. In this, the Anabaptists differed with classical Protestantism.

Among the principal hermeneutic keys that Anabaptists used for interpreting the Bible were the following: 1) the active participation of the Holy Spirit; 2) discernment in the context of the assembled community of believers; and

3) a desire for faithful and obedient ways to follow Jesus daily as his disciples.

This dependence on the intervention of the Spirit in biblical interpretation meant that some Anabaptist interpretations were not always as literal as many of their contemporaries in other traditions—and sometimes even their brothers and sisters within the movement—might have wished. For example, Anabaptist anticlericalism, along with their affirmation of the basic equality of all the members of the community of faith, was based more on a spiritual reading of the Scriptures than a strictly literal understanding of the objective words of Scripture. The same could be said of the Anabaptist willingness to recognize the ministries of women in their communities of faith. On this point they differed markedly from the established churches of the period, both Catholic and Protestant.

Virtually all Christians in the sixteenth century thought that they were living in the End Times. The Anabaptists conceived of the era in which they were living as the time when God was going to pour out His Spirit upon all flesh. Because of this strong emphasis on the activity of the Holy Spirit, the Anabaptists were always open—to some degree at least—to the possibility of progressive revelation on the part of the Spirit. They believed that they were living in a radically new historical epoch, the age of the Spirit that would precede the end of the ages. This vision enabled them to interpret the suffering they endured at the hands of their persecutors as the "birth pains" they assumed would necessarily precede the end of history.

A SPIRITUALITY THAT ENVISIONS THE CHURCH AS COMMUNITY

In their vision of the church, sixteenth-century Anabaptists differed notably from the commonly held understandings of both Catholicism and classical Protestantism. Catholicism defined the church as a "sacramental communion," or a community of salvation in which God's grace was communicated through the sacraments of the church. Classical Protestantism defined the true church by its proclamation of the gospel in its purity and the proper celebration of the sacraments.

According to both definitions, the true church was essentially invisible, made up of the elect, known only to God. The true church, in these formulations, is primarily a future reality that will be visible only at the end of time. In this, Catholics and Protestants alike perpetuated the Augustinian legacy that had emerged out of the church's conflict with the Donatists in the fourth and fifth centuries.[9] All that is really required for the true church to exist, according to this vision of the church, are the clergy carrying out their appointed roles.

In sharp contrast to this, the Anabaptists insisted that the true church is a concrete and visible community, the Body of Christ present in the world. To a considerable degree this visible, embodied ecclesiology determined the tangible forms with which Anabaptist spirituality was expressed.

In their definition of the true church, the Anabaptists often resorted to longer lists of characteristics than those employed by theologians in the established churches. Interestingly enough, it was Martin Luther who, without intending to do so, provided one of the earliest definitions of a Believers Church.[10] Luther's early understanding of the church included the following elements: 1) a community in which participation is free and uncoerced; 2) a community of faith and life; 3) a community dedicated to mutual edification and mission; 4) a community of mutual accountability; 5) a community of generous sharing; and 6) a community of the Spirit.

Menno Simons, the sixteenth-century radical reformer from the Low Countries, offered a remarkably similar list of characteristics. According to Menno, the true church was marked by: 1) "the salutary and unadulterated doctrine of His holy and divine Word;" 2) "the right and Scriptural use of the sacraments of Christ;" 3) "obedience to the holy Word . . . in Christian life which is of God;" 4) "sincere and unfeigned love for one's neighbor;" 5) "the name, will, Word and ordinance of Christ . . . confidently confessed in the face of all cruelty, tyranny, tumult, fire, sword, and violence of the world;" and 6) "the pressing cross of Christ, which is borne for the sake of His testimony and Word."[11]

Among other things, these lists suggest that it is not a simple task to define the nature and mission of the true church. In the case of the sixteenth-century Anabaptists, the ecclesial symbols or signs with which they expressed their vision of the church provide a clearer understanding of their communal spirituality. These signs are baptism, giving and receiving counsel, the Lord's Supper and mutual aid.

1. Baptism

The term "Anabaptist" (= "rebaptizers") was originally intended as an insult against the movement by their sixteenth-century adversaries. The Anabaptists themselves would have preferred a name like "brothers and sisters." But by their choice of "Anabaptist" their enemies correctly identified the fundamental issue in the debate.

The temptation among Anabaptists to spiritualize the sign of water baptism was very real—doing so would have meant the difference between life and death in the sixteenth century. Yet if members of the movement would have simply been content to emphasize only the inner baptism of the Spirit without the external baptism in water, the Anabaptist movement would not have survived. It was their persistent insistence on the necessity of this outward sign, together with the social and spiritual realities that it symbolized, that assured the existence of a visible alternative ecclesiology that we have come to know in the history of the Christian church as Anabaptism. For the Anabaptists, the inner baptism of the Spirit called for an outward and visible sign—water baptism. For them baptism carried the following meanings: 1) a public confession of their sin, together with a declaration of repentance, in the presence of a confessing congregation; 2) a testimony to faith in Christ's forgiveness of sin; 3) an incorporation into the communion of the church; 4) a shared commitment to mutual sharing and to give and receive fraternal counsel; and 5) a commission to participate in God's saving mission in the world.

The early Anabaptists were the first ecclesial community in 1000 years—at least since the time of Constantine—to directly and explicitly relate the baptismal vows of believers with the missional vocation of the church. In contrast to the practice of the missionary orders within Catholicism—where the missional calling was limited to those upon whom the "orders" of the church had been conferred—the Anabaptists insisted that the "great commission" of Jesus applied to every member of the community by virtue of the baptismal vows that they had freely assumed.

Water baptism was also a sign of "yieldedness" (*Gelassenheit*). Included in the concept of yieldedness, borrowed from late medieval Catholic mysticism, were the following themes: 1) an inner commitment to Christ and his cause; 2) a commitment to the Body of Christ, the church, with all that one is and all that one possesses ("be subject to one another out of reverence for Christ"); 3) a commitment to suffer for the love of Christ and for their brothers and sisters.

Baptism meant a transfer of one's citizenship in this world, with its values and loyalties, to citizenship in another world—the Body of Christ, the church, with its distinctive set of values and loyalties. It meant a fundamental change of kingdoms and of lords.

When authorities interrogated imprisoned Anabaptists about the reasons for their baptism the response was generally quite simple. They baptized out of an obedience to the biblical order in which belief comes *before* baptism — "believe and be baptized for the remission of your sins" (Mk. 16:16).

For the Anabaptists, baptism was fundamentally a public commitment entered into freely before the community of believers. This commitment was the basis for their promise to follow Jesus faithfully in the context of the community of believers. Thus, baptism was the outward sign of an inner transformation and a public commitment to follow Christ. The "obedience of faith" it symbolized included not only the inner testimony of the Spirit, but also an outward testimony and commitment to a new life in community, entered into together with other brothers and sisters who had made the same vows.

The Anabaptist understanding of salvation was therefore essentially corporate — social and relational rather than simply an inner and personal matter focused purely on the individual. For them, the true church was a visible community characterized by outward signs of an inward transformation. Thanks to their insistence that inner spiritual realities could not be separated from their outward expressions Anabaptism became a social movement.

2. *Fraternal Counsel*

Sixteenth-century Anabaptists understood the teachings of Jesus in Matthew 18:15-20 regarding disagreements in the community as recorded to be an evangelical, nonviolent, and compassionate alternative to the traditional manner of dealing with conflicts. In sixteenth-century society, conflicts were resolved either by the state, in the exercise of its power to impose physical punishment, or by the established churches, in their power to punish offenders by imposing ecclesiastical penalties or by turning them over to the secular powers for punishment.

Although the spiritual heirs of the sixteenth-century Anabaptists have not always been consistent in practice, their approach to correcting or punishing the wrong doer was very different. From the Anabaptist perspective, the church's discipline consisted primarily in helping each brother or sister truly become the disciple of Jesus that they affirmed in their baptismal vows. The visible similarities between the terms "disciple" and "discipline" further underscore the logic of this connection.

For the sixteenth-century Anabaptists the restoration of the true church would not be complete until its members had freely committed themselves, through their baptism, to become this kind of community, sustained by the practice of fraternal and restorative discipline.

The purpose of this approach to discipline was not punitive or aimed at excluding the offender, but rather an expression of authentic evangelization. According to

Balthasar Hubmaier, the offender was to be received again "joyfully, like a father receives a lost son" (Lk. 15).[12]

For this kind of discipline to function, the congregation needed to agree that a person's outward actions were a faithful reflection of their inward condition. If a saving faith is, in its essence, known only to God, it would be invisible. Therefore, it would not make sense to exercise mutual discipline. But if we believe that the inner and the outer expressions of human experience and action are two sides of the same coin, the exercise of mutual discipline can be truly restorative. The practice of Anabaptist discipline replaced the traditional ritual of confession, contrition, penitence and absolution within Catholicism. Lutherans, for their part, hoped that the proclamation of the Word in its purity would have this effect. In contrast to both Catholic and Protestant understandings, Anabaptists believed that outward actions faithfully reflect inner commitments and therefore called for mutual accountability.

Viewed from a congregational perspective, discipline can be understood as the concrete form that the grace of God takes in the process of continually restoring wholeness to relationships within the community of faith.

3. The Lord's Supper

The Anabaptists understood the Lord's Supper as a commemoration of the sacrificial death of Christ. In this they were the ideological heirs of a deep medieval anti-sacramental tradition expressed most vigorously in the sixteenth century by the humanist Desiderius Erasmus and the Swiss reformer, Ulrich Zwingli. But this basic understanding by no means exhausts the meaning of this symbol for the Anabaptists.

Even before the formal beginnings of the Anabaptist movement, dissidents in Switzerland—inspired initially by Zwingli's program of reforms, but later increasingly frustrated by his compromise with the civil authorities in putting those reforms into practice—had formulated some ideas that would radically "desacralize" the Lord's Supper.

Some four months before the first Anabaptist baptisms in January of 1525, several of Zwingli's closest disciples had referred to the celebration of the Lord's Supper in the following terms:

> Ordinary bread ought to be used, without idols and additions. . . . An ordinary drinking vessel too ought to be used. . . . Although it is simply bread, yet if faith and brotherly love precede it, it is to be received with joy, since it is used in the church, it is to show that we are truly one bread and one body, and that we are and wish to be true brethren with one another. . . . [We] should be willing to live and suffer for the sake of Christ and the brethren. . . . The supper is an expression of fellowship, not a Mass and sacrament. . . Neither is it to be used in "temples" . . . since that creates a false reverence. It should be used much and often.[13]

For his part, Balthasar Hubmaier wrote:

> whoever now observes the Supper of Christ . . . and regards the suffering of Christ in firm faith, the same

will also thank God for this grace and goodness and will surrender himself to the will of Christ, which is what he has done for us. We also now should make our life, body, material goods and blood available to the neighbor. That is the will of Christ.[14]

This strong emphasis on horizontal relationships was widely held among the Anabaptists. We find a similar interpretation in the *Congregational Order*, an outline of worship that likely originated in the circles associated with Michael Sattler:

The Lord's Supper shall be held, as often as the brothers are together, thereby proclaiming the death of the Lord, and thereby warning each one to commemorate, how Christ gave His life for us, and shed His blood for us, that we might also be willing to give our body and life for Christ's sake, which means for the sake of all the brothers.[15]

A common English translation of the central texts related to the Lord's Supper reads as follows: "… 'This is my body that is broken for you. *Do this* in remembrance of me.' In the same way he took the cup also after supper, saying, 'this cup is the new covenant in my blood. *Do this* as often as you drink it in remembrance of me'" (I Cor. 11:24b-25 and Lk. 22:19). We have traditionally imagined that the antecedent of "do this" was simply the practice of celebrating the Lord's Supper—that is, eat bread and drink from my cup. In contrast to this interpretation, the translation offered by the *Nueva Biblia Española*, of I Corinthians 11:23-24 provides a clearer understanding of the texts: "'This is my body, that is given for you; do *the same* in my memory,'"—that is, imitate me in this act of self-sacrificing love. Those of us accustomed to traditional interpretations of the Lord's Supper may be surprised by this translation. However, it agrees perfectly with the radical Anabaptist understanding of the Lord's Supper that we have just noted. Early Anabaptists, as well as the early Christian church, understood that both the practice of the Lord's Supper and a readiness to give ourselves on behalf of others were essential to the church's on-going life.

In water baptism we testify to the fact that we have taken seriously the biblical command to love God above all else—that we have died unto ourselves and have risen to newness of life in Christ Jesus. In the Lord's Supper we also give testimony to the fact that we have taken seriously the biblical command to love our neighbor as ourselves. This horizontal orientation of the Lord's Supper—as a response to the grace of God and as a commitment to love as God loves—is distinctly Anabaptist.

4. Mutual Aid

From the very beginnings of the Anabaptist movement, participation in the Body of Christ implied absolute loyalty to Christ in our social, economic and political relationships, which, of course, are also spiritual matters in the context of the community of faith.

Life within Anabaptist communities was inspired and enabled by the Spirit of Christ and ordered according to the model of Jesus and his disciples. It also meant that economic relationships among sixteenth-century Anabaptists would be different from those of the world. Among the Hutterian Brethren, for example, economic relationships were structured systematically around the principle of shared possessions, or a community of goods. Economic relationships among the Swiss-South German communities were less formally structured, but no less real. Both groups affirmed the same commitment to mutual aid, the same attitude of detachment from material possessions, and the same motivating Spirit. And both groups were judged by civil authorities to be a threat to the socio-economic system and were persecuted, among other charges, as dangerous "communists" and "fanatics."

Article 5 of the "Congregational Order" summarizes economic relationships among the Swiss-South German Anabaptist communities:

> Of all the brothers and sisters in this congregation none shall have anything of his own, but rather, as the Christians in the time of the apostles, held all things in common, and especially stored up a common fund, from which aid can be given to the poor, according as each will have need, and as in the apostles' time permit no brother to be in need.[16]

The Anabaptists also rejected the traditional hierarchical distinctions that characterized sixteenth-century society. They abandoned the use of honorary titles in referring to each another, including those who exercised some form of ministry within the communities. A letter by Conrad

Grebel to Thomas Müntzer, written in September of 1524, reflects this conviction:

> Dear Brother Thomas: For God's sake do not marvel that we address you without title and request thee like a brother to communicate with us by writing, and that we have ventured, unmasked and unknown to thee, to open communications between us. God's Son, Jesus Christ, . . . bids us be brethren by the one common word given to all brethren and believers. [He] has moved us and compelled us to make friendship and brotherhood.[17]

Müntzer, like Grebel, held a Master's degree, but the Anabaptists intentionally avoided honorary titles in referring to one another, since doing so would have perpetuated the social distinctions that separated the clergy from the laity as well as the educated from the uneducated.

Spirituality in Sixteenth-Century Anabaptism
Part II

A CHRIST-CENTERED SPIRITUALITY

As with many other renewal movements throughout the church's history, the person of Jesus Christ was central to the spirituality of sixteenth-century Anabaptists. Virtually all of their doctrinal formulations were orthodox, consistent with those beliefs expressed in the historic creeds of Christendom. However, one important dimension of Anabaptist Christology not emphasized in the mainstream tradition of the established churches, was the significance of Jesus as a model to be followed in daily life. In this the Anabaptists attempted to recover the reality of Christ's humanity, expressed in his words and actions, without ignoring or neglecting his divine nature.

Despite some early tendencies—especially in the Low Countries—toward docetism (the idea that Jesus in his suffering only appeared to be human) and monophysitism (the idea that Jesus had only one nature, the divine), the Anabaptist movement was characterized by a Christology strongly rooted in the Incarnation. The spirituality that emerged from this was a spirituality of discipleship.

In contrast to sixteenth-century Catholics and the classical Protestant tradition, the Anabaptists resisted the temptation to separate law from gospel, or sanctification from justification, or faith from works, or discipleship from evangelization. In a context that understood Jesus primarily as "the Savior who dies" or as "the coming Judge," the Anabaptists confessed Jesus as "the Lord to be followed."

This commitment to following Jesus—a conviction based on an incarnational Christology—had more in common with earlier radical renewal movements, both within and without the Catholic Church, than it did with the emerging Protestantism of its day. The Anabaptist commitment to imitating Jesus was similar to that of the early Franciscans and the Waldensians of the twelfth century and to the Czech Brethren of the fifteenth century.

However, the Anabaptists expressed a deepening of this conviction in both vision and practice. In addition to imitating Jesus in concrete (and sometimes legalistic) ways, the Anabaptist understood their ethical decisions to be directed by the Spirit of Christ. This understanding of discipleship as *participation* in the very nature of Jesus meant: 1) that radical discipleship would be possible, since Jesus himself had lived it out; and 2) that the words of Jesus had an authoritative meaning since Jesus himself had incarnated them. Therefore, a radically Christian life was not an impossible ideal—as sixteenth-century Christendom generally held—but a real possibility.

It is probably not an exaggeration to say that Anabaptist spirituality was a "spirituality of discipleship." For that reason they assigned great importance to biblical teachings such as the Sermon on the Mount (Mt. 5-7) and the Fruits of the Spirit (Gal. 5:13-26), in contrast to other movements, which tended to regard these passages as "law." For the Anabaptists, following Jesus in radical discipleship was the concrete expression of their experience of God's grace in their midst.

A SPIRITUALITY OF JUSTICE AND PEACE

In their desire to follow Jesus, the majority of the Anabaptists committed themselves to a nonviolent path of love and peace. They found nothing in the New Testament to justify their participation in the wars of their time or in other forms of coercive violence. For this reason, with few exceptions, they were hesitant to participate in the political structures of their day. Most believed in the reality of two distinct kingdoms: the kingdom of this world, which operates in conditions of sin, violence and human law; and the kingdom of Christ characterized by grace and the gospel, and expressed most clearly by the qualities of life in the community of faith.

In the sixteenth century many Anabaptists were persecuted and suffered injustices of all kinds. Nevertheless, they generally enjoyed popular support, although this was often hidden out of fear of the civil authorities. They were pioneers in the struggle for human rights in economics as well as in their opposition to broader forms of violence and oppression in their time such as social hierarchies, feudal inequalities, economic oppression, warfare, and the death penalty. The implications of the gospel in questions of justice, peace and "nonresistance"—as they were accustomed to calling it, taking their cue from the term that appears in Jesus' teaching: "Do not resist an evildoer" (Mt. 5:39)—were not equally evident to all Anabaptists at the outset of the movement. However, many quickly realized the importance of the Sermon on the Mount for their lives. The following citations are representative of early Anabaptist thought and action.

The first comes from Conrad Grebel and his circle. It is part of a letter dated September 5, 1524, addressed to Thomas Müntzer, a German mystic and revolutionary living in territories under the control of Lutheran authorities. For Grebel and his friends the church was to be established on nothing more or less than the principles of "the rule of Christ" (Mt. 18:15-20). This meant that coercion had no place within the community of faith. Whereas dissidents within the established churches were judged, condemned, and turned over the secular authorities for torture, imprisonment and execution, Grebel urged Müntzer to use only "determination and common prayer and decision according to faith and love, without command or compulsion."[18] "Moreover," he continued,

> the gospel and its adherents are not to be protected by the sword, nor are they thus to protect themselves, which, as we learn from our brother, is thy opinion and practice. True Christian believers are sheep among wolves, sheep for the slaughter; they must be baptized in anguish and affliction, tribulation, persecution, suffering and death; they must be tried

with fire, and must reach the fatherland of eternal rest, not by killing their bodily enemies, but by mortifying their spiritual enemies. Neither do they use the worldly sword or war, since all killing has ceased with them—unless, indeed, we would still be in the old law. And even there [in the Old Testament], so far as we recall, war was a misfortune after they had once conquered the Promised Land.[19]

This same vision was confirmed almost three years later in an Anabaptist synod held in the Swiss village of Schleitheim in February 24, 1527.

We have been united as follows concerning the sword. The sword is an ordering of God outside the perfection of Christ. It punishes and kills the wicked, and guards and protects the good. . . . But within the perfection of Christ only the ban is used for the admonition and exclusion of the one who has sinned, without the death of the flesh, simply the warning and the command to sin no more. Now many, who do not understand Christ's will for us, will ask whether a Christian may or should use the sword against the wicked for the protection and defense of the good, or for the sake of love. [Here the "just war" is in view.] The answer is unanimously revealed: Christ teaches and commands us to learn from Him, for He is meek and lowly of heart and thus we shall find rest for our souls. . . . The weapons of their battle and warfare are carnal and only against the flesh, but the weapons of Christians are spiritual, against the fortification of the devil. The worldly are armed with steel and iron, but Christians are armed with the armor of God, with truth, righteousness, peace, faith, salvation, and with the Word of God.[20]

Only three months after the Anabaptist meeting at Schleitheim, Michael Sattler, one of the principal participants, was judged and sentenced to an unimaginably cruel form of torture and execution. The list of the charges against Sattler provides a glimpse of the Anabaptist attitude regarding civil authority and the various forms of human violence.

1) That he and his associates have acted against the imperial mandate. . . ; 6) [he] said that one should not swear to the government. . . ; 9) He has said: "If the Turk were to come into the land, one should not resist him," and, "if it were right to wage war, [he] would rather go to war against the Christians than against the Turks," which is after all a great offense, to take the side of the greatest enemy of our holy faith against us.[21]

Later, in his own defense, Michael Sattler added:

If the Turk comes, he should not be resisted, for it stands written: thou shalt not kill. We should not defend ourselves against the Turks or our other persecutors, but with fervent prayer should implore God that He might be our defense and our resistance. As to the saying that if waging war were proper I would rather take the field against the so-called Christians who persecute, take captive, and kill true

Christians, than against the Turks, this was for the following reason: the Turk is a genuine Turk and knows nothing of the Christian faith. He is a Turk according to the flesh. But you claim to be Christians, boast of Christ, and still persecute the faithful witnesses of Christ. Thus you are Turks according to the Spirit.[22]

Menno Simons, who provided the leadership essential to the survival of the Anabaptist movement in the Low Countries during the decades following a violent and disastrous uprising of Anabaptists in Münster in 1535, provides testimony in his writings on themes of justice, peace and nonviolence that is very similar to that which we have noted in the Swiss and South German movement.

No, dear sirs, no, [bloodshed] will not be able to free you in the judgment day of God (Lk 22:50). . . . They know no other weapons except patience, hope, silence, and God's Word (Mt. 10:14; Is. 30:15). The weapons of our knighthood, says Paul, are not fleshly but mighty before God to destroy all attacks, overthrowing everything which lifts itself up against the knowledge of God, and taking all understanding captive to the obedience of Christ (2 Cor. 10:4-5).[23]

Nor did Menno Simons hesitate to bear witness to civil authorities who claimed to be Christians:

I agree wholeheartedly that the office of magistrate is of God and His order. But I hate those who are Christian, and want to be one, and then do not follow their prince, head, and leader, Christ, but cover and clothe their unrighteousness, wickedness, pomp and pride, avarice, greed, and tyranny with the name of magistrate. For those who are Christian must follow the Spirit, Word and example of Christ, whether they are emperor, king, or whoever.[24]

In the early 1530s Jacob Hutter emerged as a leader among the pacifist Anabaptist community in Moravia. The ruling nobles were generally well-disposed toward the Anabaptists, thanks to the economic benefits they brought to their territories, and were willing to grant them favors and protect them in the face of Imperial decrees ordering their persecution. However Hutter was resolute in his resistance to the nobles when they ordered the Anabaptists to pay taxes in order to finance the Empire's wars against the Turks.

Therefore [God] has also arranged that every government collect annual taxes or interest or rent that they may be able to carry on their office, and if someone would resist this, they would be found against the order of God. . . . Therefore we too have never resisted this, as obedient subjects of human ordinances, for the sake of the Lord. However, where one departs from this order and against God, or not ordered by God, and seeks annual taxes for war or hangman's pay or other things which are not proper for a Christian or have no basis in Scripture, but rather are against God and His Son, to that we cannot consent. [Christ] did not come to condemn souls but to save them, not to return evil for evil, or blow for blow, but rather to repay evil with good, to show the nature of our Father in heaven by doing good to our enemies."[25]

In a document from 1642, the Anabaptists clearly declared that these principles of peace and nonviolence should be applied to the full range of human relationships.

One [should] always act toward the poor as one would have God act toward us (Col 4:4). . . . Often persons are so harsh toward a neighbor, when they are to forgive them something, asking for a great confession of guilt before they can be forgiven. When they divide an inheritance, they are so shrewd that they want to make certain to receive their own share and not be generous simply for the sake of peace. The same with buying things; they disregard the seller and concentrate upon the wares they are buying, not thinking about whether their neighbor earns anything in the process; yet when they have something to sell they place the price so high, and hardly know how to stop praising their wares. This is true greed, self-love, and unrighteousness. So also the laborer often desires big wages while doing little work, or only half the work expected for it. This all comes from an impure heart which has no compassion for the neighbor."[26]

Andreas Ehrenpreis, one of the last significant leaders of the Hutterian Brethren in Moravia, writing in 1650, emphasized the economic dimensions of a common life shared together in a radical community, a life characterized by justice and peace.

Whoever claims to belong to Christ in love, but cannot give their possessions to the community for the sake of Christ and the poor, cannot deny that they love worldly goods, over which they have only been placed as caretakers for a time. Therefore Christ says, blessed are the poor in spirit, for theirs is the kingdom of heaven (Mt 5:3). Yet Christ does not ask this simply for the sake of the poor, but also that his followers may be free and surrendered [*gelassen* = yielded; at peace] and not have a treasure on earth to which they tie their heart. . . . Let everyone seek the welfare of others.[27]

A SPIRITUALITY OF MISSIONAL VOCATION

Within sixteenth-century European Christendom there was very little sense of missional vocation—for a very simple reason. With the exception of a few Muslims and a Jewish minority the entire population of Europe had already been "christened" through infant baptism.

With the "discovery" of the New World new missionary orders emerged within European Catholicism. While the Franciscans and the Dominicans were "christianizing" the pagan peoples of the Western Hemisphere, the armed forces of the Catholic, Lutheran and Reformed countries of Europe were waging war against each other to determine which of the three groups would become the established church. What resulted was a political, rather than a religious, solution. Under the principle of *cuius regio, euius religio* ("whose region, his religion") the religious affiliation of the ruler would automatically become that of the people. It was not until the Pietist revival at the end of the seventeenth century that a new sense of missional vocation emerged among classical Protestants. Even then, interest in mission arose primarily among the Pietists, on the margins of Christendom, outside the official ecclesiastical structures.

By contrast, the Anabaptist movement understood its vocation in missional terms already in the sixteenth century. Indeed, the Great Commission was one of their favorite texts. In their vision of the church, they considered themselves to be living in the era in which "the Lord's house shall be established as the highest of the mountains," when "the nations of the earth will learn to walk in the ways of the Lord and God's law shall go out through all the earth" (Mi. 4:1-4).[28] Another favorite Anabaptist missionary texts was Psalm 24:1: "The earth is the Lord's and all that is in it, the world, and those who live in it." With this confident claim they felt authorized to evangelize anywhere and everywhere, even though it was forbidden by the established church and secular authorities.

Anabaptists in the sixteenth century were therefore forced to pursue their evangelizing mission outside existing legal structures. Remarkably, however, they not only survived as a hidden church, they also successfully evangelized under extremely adverse conditions. Work places soon became favorite locations for evangelical activity. And even in very difficult situations and within a highly patriarchal world, it was women who often became the most effective evangelizers—indeed, fully one-third of the early Anabaptist martyrs were women.

Thus, without recourse to socio-political, economic or religious power—and without access to public means of communication such as official edicts and laws, the printing press, or higher education—the Anabaptists evangelized from the margins, witnessing to their faith "from below" by means of personal conversation, backed by the integrity of their life (and death!). In this process they subverted, in the name of God's reign of justice, the oppressive kingdoms of their time.

To conclude: the spirituality of the sixteenth-century Anabaptists, like that of the Christians of the first century, was characterized by the following elements: 1) it was inspired by the spirit of the Living Christ; 2) it was oriented by the Scriptures, read and interpreted in the faith community; 3) it was consciously corporate—nourished and shared in the context of the community; 4) it was a Christ-centered spirituality of discipleship in which following Jesus was not the privilege of an unusually committed minority, nor reserved for a "spiritual" elite, but the calling of the entire community of Christ; 5) it was a spirituality characterized by a commitment to justice and peace in every aspect of life, as understood in the biblical term, Shalom; and 6) it was a spirituality that expressed itself by participating fully in God's saving mission in the world, a mission that anticipated, announced and embodied the reign of God in this world.

Spiritualities in Dialogue in the 21st Century:
Anabaptists in Conversation with Others

John Howard Yoder, a well-known Mennonite theologian, has observed that radical reform movements tend to take on the mirror image of the very deficiencies that they have identified and are attempting to reform in the established churches.

For example, in a context where the church defined itself as a "sacramental communion," the radicals tended to eliminate the sacramental dimension from their ecclesiology in the hopes of recovering a dynamic vision and practice more relevant to their historical setting. Thus, in their reaction against an "idolatrous" liturgy, sixteenth-century Anabaptist worship deprived itself of some of the rich symbolism through which God's grace and love are communicated.[29]

However, in this desire to respond more faithfully to the gospel, the Anabaptists have not been the only ones in the history of the church whose spirituality has been impoverished. Roland Bainton, a renowned twentieth-century church historian, once suggested that Martin Luther's greatest tragedy consisted in not having Anabaptists nearby with whom to engage in meaningful dialogue. At the same time, in their reaction against Luther's resolute emphasis on "justification by faith alone,

61

without works" — and the almost inevitable lowering of ethical standards such an emphasis entailed — some Anabaptist groups emphasized obedience to the teachings of Christ so strongly, indeed almost exclusively, that they sometimes became victims of a sort of moral paralysis or legalism. This tension has lasted for many generations among some Anabaptist-Mennonite congregations.

In the introduction and conclusion to his book *From Anabaptist Seed*, the Canadian Mennonite historian, Arnold Snyder, offers an image that is both simple and profound in its reflection on the necessity for every spirituality to be accompanied by a particular identity.

> All farmers know that in order to grow healthy plants that bear fruit, three things are necessary: good seed, good soil and careful cultivation. The choice of the seed is crucial. Anyone who plants a mango seed and hopes to harvest oranges will be very disappointed. No amount of fertilizer will change the nature of the plant, contained as it was in the seed. But choosing and planting the right seed is not sufficient. The seed must be planted in fertile ground, or it withers and dies; and the young plants must be nourished and cared for, if one expects to harvest fruit.

> Think of our churches as plants. Our church family first saw the light in the sixteenth century. It sprang from an Anabaptist seed. That original seed found fertile soil, was cultivated and nurtured, and produced an abundant harvest. The seeds of that harvest have been transplanted throughout the world

now for almost 500 years. The basic nature of the seed is still visible in the plant, although cultivation and different climates have also changed the plant in important ways.

At the same time, however, Snyder also encourages us to continually take up the task of entering anew into fellowship and dialogue with Christians of other traditions regarding our respective spiritualities.

> There is much that we can and should learn from the testimony of these faithful witnesses. Nevertheless, one seed alone cannot be expected to fill God's entire vineyard. One variety of grape cannot provide every kind of wine, from sweet to dry, red to white.[30]

In the sixteenth-century, Christians generally held the conviction that there was only one truth, and that this, of necessity, was to be found in only one tradition. For that reason, the established churches—who believed that they were the custodians of this truth—persecuted and even executed those in the reform movements who dared to question their authority. Yet ironic as it may seem, once they had consolidated their existence and established their identity, these same reform movements, tended to assume a similar attitude toward their adversaries.

Thanks, in part at least, to the contributions of some of these radical reform movements—who assumed that God would continue to reveal His will and that we might continue to discover new truths from His Holy Word—we are learning to appreciate the wide variety of gifts and legacies that have been preserved by each of the Christian traditions. As heirs of the Anabaptist tradition we also have valuable elements to contribute to this dialogue, even as we continue to learn from others.

In the remainder of this chapter we will seek to summarize some of the essential dimensions of Anabaptist spirituality as described in Chapters 3 and 4. Then, in light of the experiences that Anabaptists and other traditions have shared from the sixteenth century to the present, we suggest the following ways in which we can be mutually enriched as we enter into dialogue with other Christians and their distinctive spiritualities.

1. Pneumatology

In the context of established forms of Christendom in the sixteenth century, both Catholic and Protestant, the Anabaptist recovery of the Holy Spirit in their personal and community life proved to be life-giving. Their experience of three baptisms—of the Spirit, of water, and of blood—symbolized the depth and intensity of their encounter with God and with their neighbor. This was not only true in the sixteenth century, but throughout their history as they participated in God's mission in the world.

Some contemporary Anabaptists, however, have needed to experience this reality anew, through the gifts we have received from other traditions and other spiritualities. For example, thanks especially to the contributions of pentecostal and charismatic Christians some of us have remembered and experienced afresh aspects of our spiritual tradition that had gone forgotten in our practice.

2. *Biblical Authority and Interpretation*

In the context of Christendom, where the established tradition recognized the absolute authority of the church's hierarchy in matters of moral discernment and biblical interpretation, the "hermeneutic community" that characterized Anabaptists in the sixteenth century was virtually unique.

It was largely the Catholic church's controversies with dissidents during their history that led to the almost absolute authority of the church's teaching office, or magisterium. Among Catholics this function was exercised by the bishops and, in the last resort, by the bishop of Rome—the pope. Among the Lutherans and other Protestants, the professors of theology in their universities and the clergy exercised this function, with the understanding that ultimately the prince was the highest bishop (*summus episcopus*) of the church in each territory.

For their part, the early Anabaptists felt that the will of God could be discerned and the Scriptures interpreted: 1) within the community of disciples committed to knowing and following God's will in their life and mission; 2) in their study of Scripture through which God continued to reveal Himself; 3) as they gathered together under the inspiration and direction of the Holy Spirit present in their midst; and 4) in their commitment to put God's will for them into practice.

3. *Ecclesiology*

In a context where the marks of the true church were understood largely in static or abstract categories—such as a "sacramental communion (Catholic), a custodian of sound doctrine and worship practices (Reformed), or "where the Word is preached in truth and the sacraments are celebrated correctly" (Luther)—the Anabaptist vision of the church was outrageously bold. The Anabaptists viewed the church as the community of brothers and sisters authorized to interpret Scripture in order to practice the "rule of Christ," that is, to communicate God's forgiveness by restoring the errant brother or sister. In fact, Hubmaier and Grebel both regarded a commitment to practice and this new understanding of the church as an essential requirement for the baptism of new believers.

In Anabaptist ecclesiology describing the marks of the true church required a longer list than was true of Catholics or classical Protestants. Menno Simons is a good example. For Menno, the true church consisted of: 1) "the salutary and unadulterated doctrine of His holy and divine Word;" 2) "the right and Scriptural use of the sacraments of Christ;" 3) "obedience to the holy Word . . . in Christian life which is of God;" 4) "sincere and unfeigned love for one's neighbor;" 5) "the name, will, Word and ordinance of Christ . . . confidently confessed in the face of all cruelty, tyranny, tumult, fire, sword, and violence of the world;" and 6) "the pressing cross of Christ, which is borne for the sake of His testimony and Word."[31]

4. Christology and Soteriology

For the Anabaptists, salvation did not depend exclusively on the inner faith of the believer. Key phrases in the Schleitheim Confession include "the obedience of faith" and a call "to walk in the resurrection of Jesus Christ."[32] According to this vision, salvation is essentially relational and therefore inseparable from ecclesiology. Salvation implies radical communion with both God and neighbor and is incarnated in a Christ-like life in the community of faith. The soteriology of Michael Sattler, for example, synthesizes both Catholic and classical Protestant elements. In reality, however, this vision of salvation in the context of community was neither Catholic nor Protestant, but distinctly Anabaptist. Salvation is personal, but it is not fundamentally individualistic in the sense of a person being able to experience it independently of a community of faith. Reconciliation with God is always accompanied by reconciliation with the neighbor. To follow Jesus was to truly know him. The Anabaptist concepts and practices of discipleship were derived from their Christology.

In an environment in which Jesus was primarily understood as "a coming Judge" or as " a Savior who died," early Anabaptists confessed Jesus as "Lord to be followed" in all dimensions of their daily life.

5. Justice and Peace

Since the fourth century—when the Roman emperor Constantine facilitated the close relationship between the state and the church that has come to characterize subsequent Christian history and the corresponding emergence of Augustine's defense of Christian participation in warfare (the so-called "Just War")—the peace witness of the Church has been divided. We have not been able to witness to the world with one voice on matters of justice and peace. Instead, established Christianity has sought to clarify when and under what circumstances Christians might be able to participate in warfare without sinning, thereby limiting, in theory at least, violence among Christians but nonetheless justifying the practice of lethal violence.

However, this was not always the case for Christians. Among the earliest church fathers whose writings have been preserved, none justified the participation of Christians in warfare. The great majority of Christians in the pre-Constantinian church, as well as many of the radical reform movements within the church from Constantine to our own times, proclaimed with words and deeds their opposition to all forms of Christian violence.

On questions of war and peace, the mainstream churches—Orthodox, Catholics and Protestants alike—have generally recognized their indebtedness to the radical reform movements and have come to expect from Anabaptists a witness and practice that promote relationships of justice and peace. In these times of "wars and rumors of wars" it is crucial that we nourish and retain this vision among our spiritual family of brothers and sisters. For example, before the U.S. and British invasion of Iraq in 2003 it became clear that members of the Anabaptist-Mennonite family in the United States who have traditionally been absolute pacifists were no longer of one accord on matters of peace and war. In the events since the Gulf War the erosion of the peace conviction has continued find expression among Anabaptist-Mennonites.

Clearly, on-going dialogue is needed not only at an interconfessional or interdenominational level, but also within our own denominations and congregations.

In my travels throughout the Mennonite world I have observed that it is possible to maintain an *ideology* of peace, apart from any accompanying concrete practices of these ideas. But it is virtually impossible to sustain an authentic *theology* of peace in the absence of concrete practices of justice and peace. Here we note the stark difference between ideology and theology as guiding principles for our lives. Authentic theology expresses truths that are lived out in practice, so that we may understand and live them more faithfully and communicate them more clearly in our missional witness.

Many of our brothers and sisters in the global south have reminded us of the essential relationship between *justice* and *peace* in our call to participate in God's Shalom in the world. Menno Simons seems to have understood this clearly. Like the prophets of old, he understood justice in its biblical sense—as God giving us what we *need*, rather than what we *deserve*.

> All those who are born of God . . . are . . . to love their neighbors, not only with money and goods, but also after the example of their Lord and Head, Jesus Christ, in an evangelical manner, with life and blood. They show mercy and love. . . . No one among them is allowed to beg. . . . They entertain those in distress. They take the stranger into their houses. They comfort the afflicted; assist the needy; clothe the naked; feed

the hungry; do not turn their face from the poor; do not despise their own flesh.[33]

6. Missionary Vocation

Undoubtedly, one of the most original contributions of the sixteenth-century Anabaptists to the wider church was their understanding that baptism was a commissioning to participate in God's mission in the world. In contrast to the Catholic missionary orders, where the missional commission was limited to those who had formally received the "orders" (or ordination) of the church, the Anabaptists were the first ecclesial community since the time of Constantine to apply the Great Commission to all of their members on the basis of their baptismal vows. In this commitment they restored the missionary vision and practice of the first-century church.

During the course of the twentieth century, Anabaptist-Mennonites in the U.S. recovered some of the missionary vision they had lost since the sixteenth century, not so much by reclaiming their radical historical roots, but more because of the influence of other traditions and Christian spiritualities which gave rise to the Protestant mission movement. It has taken many years for this missionary vision to root itself deeply through a fresh reading of Scriptures and a rediscovery of our own radical history.

Another challenge for the descendants of the early Anabaptists is to recover the full dimensions of justice and peace in our evangelization. Here our tendency to listen more to the voices around us than to embrace a radical reading of Scriptures has led us to regard justice and peace more as a matter of Christian ethics than as qualities at the very heart of the New Testament gospel. Yet in the New Testament, the gospel is a gospel of peace!

In order to communicate the gospel authentically, Christians must love our enemies, just as God loves His enemies. "While we were still sinners," we read in Romans, "Christ died for us" (Rom. 5:8). Here we find ourselves face-to-face with the scandal of Jesus' messianic mission. Christ came proclaiming the gospel of peace to the outsiders, the disinherited, the marginalized—to all who were thought to be the adversaries of God.

We who are the heirs of the sixteenth-century Anabaptists still have much to learn from our radical brothers and sisters who participate in other Christian traditions. In our life together with brothers and sisters in the greater family of faith we do not enjoy the luxury of being able to choose our spiritual ancestors. We are all heirs of one tradition or another. The life and mission of the universal Church will be greatly blessed when all of these traditions bring their contributions to the table of fraternal communion.

Many years ago, in a conversation with Rene Padilla, a highly-respected Latin American theologian and biblical scholar, Padilla shared his conviction that our theological understanding will finally be complete only when all traditions within the Christian church have been able to bring to the table their experiences of God's grace and of God's project to restore both humanity and creation.

In the light of the enormity of the promise and challenge before us the urgent questions we face will include the following: 1) What contributions do we need to receive from our brothers and sisters in other traditions as they seek to live out God's purposes in their midst? 2) What contributions do our brothers and sisters in other traditions hope to receive from us out of our attempts to be faithful to God's call in our lives? 3) How can we all participate more faithfully in God's saving purposes, as co-participants in God's mission in the world?

Conclusion:
Radical Spirituality

In the light of the great variety of Christian spiritualities circulating today, some of which are frankly inadequate or even deformed, it is absolutely necessary that we return to our roots in Jesus and to the community inspired by his Spirit in the first century in order to re-orient our own spirituality.

In marked contrast to many traditional spiritualities, the Bible does not allow the distinctions we often make between the inner and the outer, or between the spiritual and the material, or between believing and doing. For many, Mother Theresa's community in Calcutta is an example of an authentic Christian spirituality. For Mother Theresa, to touch the untouchables was to touch the Body of Christ. To love in an utterly unselfish way was, for her, a form of prayer. She did not stop praying to serve; nor did she stop serving to pray. Authentic spirituality is all embracing.

The cross of Jesus is the clearest model of a spirituality that is authentically Christian. It is at once a sign of absolute identification with God and an expression of God's solidarity with humanity. In the cross, the spirit of Jesus is reflected most clearly. This is the spirituality that his disciples are called to practice. The cross is simultaneously the most eloquent prayer of intercession to the Father on behalf of humanity, and the clearest and the most powerful response of God to the powers of evil. In the cross of Jesus, and in the cross borne by his followers, we find the very essence of Christian spirituality.

A truly authentic Christian spirituality therefore will not be amorphous. It will take forms that are truly visible and salvific. Christian spirituality is the process of following Jesus Christ under the inspiration of the Spirit in the context of a shared life within the Messianic community. For this reason, Christian spirituality is Trinitarian: it is lived in absolute dependence on God the Father, oriented toward the model of Jesus, and empowered by the impulse and inspiration of the Holy Spirit.

A fully Christian spirituality—like that which we see reflected in the Messianic community of the first century— is, above all else, rooted in God's grace and expressed concretely in following Jesus. This means that our entire life is lived in the power of the spirit of Jesus Christ himself. An authentic Christian spirituality will be nourished and shared in the context of the community of the Living Christ. From the Biblical perspective the idea of a "solitary saint" is an impossibility.

Finally, a fully Christian spirituality will be incarnated in mission—God's mission in the world carried out with unique clarity and power by Jesus of Nazareth, as he lived under the impulse and inspiration of God's Spirit.

For those of us who share the radical Anabaptist tradition, it is especially interesting to note the points of overlap between the sixteenth-century Anabaptists and the spirituality of the early Christian community in the first century. The same could be said of the heirs of other Christian traditions, equally radical in their spirituality rooted in Jesus Christ and in the first-century Messianic community. The spirituality that characterized the Anabaptist movement depended on the powerful intervention of the Spirit of the risen Christ. But what distinguished the Anabaptists most from other traditions was undoubtedly their ecclesiological understandings and practices—participation in the Christian community was absolutely essential. The rich and varied dimensions of this participation were reflected in the four symbols of community that marked their corporate spirituality.

In *baptism* the Anabaptists committed themselves to following Christ, to "walk in the resurrection" and to live in "the obedience of faith" as they themselves confessed. But they also saw themselves as fully commissioned to participate in God's mission in the world. And this, in marked contrast with other traditions, was the privilege of all Christians, not simply of the clergy. In baptism, Anabaptists also committed themselves to receive and to offer *fraternal counsel* according to "the rule of Christ" (Mt 18:15-20), and they committed themselves to *mutual sharing*—helping one another with their material, as well as their spiritual, needs. In their celebration of the *Lord's Supper* Anabaptists renewed their vows to follow Jesus, even to the point of laying down their lives for their fellow humans, just as Jesus had done.

In their Christology, they confessed that Jesus was not only to be revered as a "Savior who dies" or as the "coming Judge," but also as the "Lord to be followed" in a life of daily discipleship. Their spirituality was marked by this vision. Their participation in the reign of God, in which Jesus was already Lord, led the Anabaptists to adopt a spirituality characterized by justice and peace, just as Jesus had proclaimed and practiced. All of this led the Anabaptists to embrace, to a remarkable degree for their time, a spirituality marked by the missional vocation implied in their understanding of baptism.

The spiritual heirs of the Radical Reformation of the sixteenth-century certainly have no monopoly on this kind of spirituality. All who are workers in the Lord's vineyard have contributions to make toward a recovery of the Christian spirituality reflected in the life of the early church. Neither orthodoxy nor heterodoxy is automatically passed on from one generation to another. Therefore every new generation has the opportunity and the responsibility to engage once again in mutual dialogue in their search for the new forms that an authentically Christian spirituality will take in their midst.

In the sense that Christian spirituality consists of following Jesus of Nazareth under the impulse of the Spirit, there is only one spirituality. However, in the sense that Christians seek to follow Jesus, each in his or her own particular historical context, there can be a diversity of Christian spiritualities. These differences are found in the variety of historical, geographical and cultural settings in which discipleship is practiced. All of our spiritualities, without exception, can be enriched—thanks be to God!—

through the contributions of brothers and sisters in other traditions.

Undoubtedly, the essential elements of authentic spirituality that we have noted in Jesus and in the early church will be of lasting validity. Among other things they will include a vital pneumatology, a corporate communal ecclesiology that is truly transforming, a Christology and soteriology that are truly salvific—that is, reconciling us with God and with our fellow humans, including our adversaries—and communal relationships marked by the justice and peace that characterize life under God's reign. This is the restored communion of the new creation that we proclaim in deed and word in the missional vocation that we share.

End Notes

1. David J. Bosch, *A Sprituality of the Road* (Scottdale, Pa.: Herald Press, 1979), 13-14.

2. Segundo Galilea, *El camino de la espiritualidad* (Buenos Aires: Paulinas, 1982), 41-44.

3. Walter Klaassen, *Anabaptism in Outline* (Scottdale, Pa.: Herald Press, 1981), 87.

4. Galilea, *El camino de la espiritualidad*, 59.

5. The principal biblical texts are Galatians 5:16-6:10 and Romans 8:1-30.

6. Hans Denck, the humanistically oriented South-German Radical Reformer, as well as Ulrich Stadler, spokesman for the Austrian Hutterian Brethren, agree on this point: "I value Holy Scripture above all human treasures but not as high as the Word of God, which is living, powerful and eternal, and which is free and unencumbered by all the elements of this world. For insofar as it [the Word] is God himself it is spirit and no letter, written without pen and paper and it may never be expunged. Therefore also salvation cannot be tied to the Scriptures, however important and good they may be with respect to it." — Klaassen, *Anabaptism in Outline*, 142. And further: "Therefore whoever wishes to use the Scripture with true reverence and not to attribute to it more than it deserves, or belongs to it, must radically separate the Scriptures and the spoken word from the inner word of the heart. . . [The outer Word] is not the living Word of God but only a letter or likeness or witness of the inner or eternal Word. This living Word is internally witnessed by the outer word if one pays close attention to it. It is like a sign on an inn which witnesses to the wine in the cellar. But the sign is not the wine. . . . The true inner Word is the eternal almighty power of God, of the same form in man as in God, which is capable of all things. It is given after perseverance in many tribulations in the discipline of the Lord. John calls this the new commandment that is true in him and in you. Only Christ under the holy cross teaches this. According to the true order of God this Word is preceded by the outer word. The preacher is to admonish by means of the external word that one should surrender and listen to the internal teacher and not allow the people to depend upon the outer word. Otherwise preachers, Scriptures and words become idols." —Ibid., 143, 145-146.

7. Quoted George H. Williams, *The Radical Reformation* (Philadelphia: Westminster Press, 1962), 823.

8. Cornelius J. Dyck, ed., *An Introduction to Mennonite History* (Scottdale, Pa.: Herald Press, 1967), 23.

9. The Donatists held that the church must be composed of saints and not sinners, and that baptisms conducted by bishops who were discovered to be traitors to the Christian cause were invalid. Augustine and the dominant Catholic tradition rejected these arguments, insisting that the purity of the church was ultimately in God's hands.

10. The following quotation is extracted from Luther's "Preface to the German Mass and Order of Service," written in 1526: "The third kind of service should be a truly evangelical order and should not be held in a public place with all sorts of people. But those who want to be Christians . . . should sign their names and meet alone in a house somewhere to pray, to read, to baptize, to receive the sacrament, and to do other Christians works. According to this order, those who de not lead Christian lives could be known, reproved, corrected, cast out, or excommunicated, according to the rule of Christ, Matthew 18 [:15-17]. Here one could also solicit benevolent gifts to be willingly given and distributed to the poor, according to St. Paul's example, 2 Corinthians 9. Here would be no need of much and elaborate singing. Here one could set up a brief and neat order for baptism and the sacrament and center everything on the Word, prayer, and love. . . . In short, if one had the kind of people and persons who wanted to be Christians in earnest, the rules and regulations would soon be ready. But as yet I neither can nor desire to begin such a congregation or assembly or to make rules for it. . . . For if I should try to make it up out of my own need, it might turn into a sect." —Ulrich S. Leupold, ed., *Liturgy and Hymns*, in *Luther's Works*, ed. Helmut T. Lehmann (Philadelphia: Fortress Press, 1965), 53:62-64.

11. *The Complete Writings of Menno Simons*, trans. Leonard Verduin, and ed. J. C. Wenger (Scottdale, Pa.: Herald Press, 1956), 739-741.

12. Klaassen, *Anabaptism in Outline*, 215.

13. Ibid., 191-192.

14. Ibid., 193.

15. *The Legacy of Michael Sattler* trans. and ed. John H. Yoder (Scottdale, Pa.: Herald Press, 1973), 45.

16. Ibid., 45.

17. *Spiritual and Anabaptist Writers*, eds. George H. Williams and Angel M. Mergal (Philadelphia: The Westminister Press, 1957), 73-74.

18. Ibid., 79.

19. Ibid., 80.

20. Yoder, *The Legacy of Michael Sattler*, 39-41.

21. Ibid., 70-71.

22. Ibid., 72-73.

23. Cornelius J. Dyck, *Spiritual Life in Anabaptism* (Scottdale, Pa.: Herald Press, 1995), 113.

24. Ibid., 114.

25. Ibid., 116.

26. Ibid., 119.

27. Ibid., 123.

28. It is interesting to note that this text was also among those most quoted by Christian writers of the first three centuries.

29. Conrad Grebel compared parts of the singing in the cathedral in Zurich with the "barking of dogs."

30. C. Arnold Snyder, *From Anabaptist Seed* (Intercourse, Pa.: Good Books, 1999), 5, 46.

31. *Complete Writings of Menno Simons*, 739-741.

32. Yoder, *The Legacy of Michael Sattler*, 36, 38.

33. *Complete Writings of Menno Simons*, 558.